In an increasingly broken world, *Woman of Valor* brings a much-needed call to action for women to be courageous. To fight not only for their personal world, but for the world around them. With an open and engaging writing style that makes for an enjoyable read, Marilynn Chadwick explores what it takes to become a woman of valor. By providing personal anecdotes and stories that are both compelling and inspiring, Marilynn discovers a common thread in the way women of valor strive to be *strong* women of God, using their gifts to influence the world. I encourage you to delve into this captivating book as Marilynn navigates the true meaning of *eshet chayil,* Woman of Valor.

—**Lauren Perdue**
Olympic gold medalist in swimming. Lauren overcame a serious injury to win gold in the 2012 Summer Olympics (*Gold and Glory*: sports writer Kevin Travis).

Woman of Valor gives us fresh insight into the Proverbs 31 woman. It's not about "becoming" the perfect P31 woman. Marilynn takes us much deeper. She takes us on a journey across generations and time zones to meet real life women who changed their corner of the world. Women who overcame rejection, poverty, disappointment and tragedy. Women who found life at its fullest when they began to give their lives away. And, through each story, she not only challenges us but also equips us to do the same. Marilynn didn't write this book as an outsider looking in. She lives this, day in and day out. She is living, breathing evidence that when we give our lives away, we get far more in return.

—**Wendy Blight**
Proverbs 31 First 5 writing team, Bible teacher, author of *I Know His Name,*
Living So That, and *Hidden Joy in a Dark Corner*

In *Woman of Valor*, Marilynn Chadwick challenges women to stand firm in their biblical role as courageous and tender warriors on behalf of others. Marilynn speaks with authenticity, since she has used her gifts and influence to fight with love on behalf of her children, her husband, and the impoverished and oppressed for more than three decades. Marilynn introduced me to Africa; an introduction that literally changed my life and has impacted the lives of countless others through the work of Fashion & Compassion. Whatever your stage of life, *Woman of Valor* will inspire you to discover the strength, courage, and hope God has given you to share with a world in need.

—**Michele Dudley**
Founder/director, Fashion & Compassion

Marilynn's gift has been to paint a picture of two sides of womanhood—feminine strength. As long as I've known Marilynn, her passion has been to empower and equip women to reflect Jesus. The pages of this book will give a refreshing view of womanhood through the eyes of unexpected, and often unsung, heroes. Whether you're in the boardroom, the classroom, the playroom or the living room, you will be stretched and strengthened to be the woman God is calling you to be and leave His mark on your world.

—**Lisa Allen**
Executive director of ministry training, Proverbs 31.
Board certified life coach.

Marilynn Chadwick's inspiring book weaves biblical stories about courageous women into everyday real life situations. Her personal stories are refreshing and revealing as she compares modern living with its many trials to those of women in the Bible. I have known Marilynn many years and can testify she is first of all, a woman who loves God with all her heart, an incredible wife and mother, and good friend.

—**Dee Ray**
Cofounder and former president of Raycom Sports Network, Inc.
Cofounder and president of Nuray Media.

WOMAN
of
VALOR

MARILYNN CHADWICK

HARVEST HOUSE PUBLISHERS
EUGENE, OREGON

Cover by Bryce Williamson, Eugene, Oregon

Cover Image © AZ / Shutterstock; OttoKrause / iStock

WOMAN OF VALOR

Published by Harvest House Publishers
Eugene, Oregon 97402
www.harvesthousepublishers.com

ISBN: 978-0-7369-7027-3 (pbk)
ISBN: 978-0-7369-7028-0 (eBook)

Library of Congress Cataloging-in-Publication Data
Names: Chadwick, Marilynn, author.
Title: Woman of valor / Marilynn Chadwick.
Description: Eugene, Oregon : Harvest House Publishers, [2017] |
Identifiers: LCCN 2017006227 (print) | LCCN 2017022941 (ebook) | ISBN
    9780736970280 (ebook) | ISBN 9780736970273 (pbk.)
Subjects: LCSH: Women—Religious aspects—Christianity. | Christian
    women—Religious life.
Classification: LCC BT704 (ebook) | LCC BT704 .C43 2017 (print) | DDC
    248.8/43—dc23
LC record available at https://lccn.loc.gov/2017006227

Printed in the United States of America

17 18 19 20 21 22 23 24 25 / BP-KBD / 10 9 8 7 6 5 4 3 2 1

To my daughter, Bethany—

It's been fun to watch you grow into a brave and beautiful woman of valor. The way you love Ryan, mother your children, and share Jesus with the world makes me so proud.

Acknowledgments

To the amazing women of valor who left their imprint on my life. Mom, you poured life into your daughters so we could reach our dreams. You have the beautiful heart of a servant. To my sisters: Susan, you've clung to your courage, compassion, and sense of humor—even while battling back from a brain injury. Janice, beneath your gentle, artistic temperament, you have incredible endurance.

To Bethany, my lovely firstborn and only daughter. You're a multi-talented leader. Friend-magnet. A world-changer raising world-changers. To my daughter-in-law Jessie: Our son DB found a treasure when he found you. I love your adventurous spirit—you've been to Africa twice and are the only one in the family to climb Mount Kilimanjaro! Soon-to-be daughter-in-law Cassi, you are adorable beyond words and so artistic. You're strong. Easy to love. Michael hasn't stopped smiling since he met you.

To my granddaughters: Anna Grace, thanks for telling me about "princesses" as only a six-year-old can. To me, you're a princess. Emily, your great love and your fierce, warrior heart will make you mighty for God. To our niece, Emily Ann: I can't wait to see where your strength and kindness will lead you. You're sure to be a difference maker.

To my dear friends serving the Lord on six continents: Krista, Kamala, Kirsten, Pamela, Bernadette, Ange, and Rosalia. Women of valor like you are one reason the gospel spreads in difficult and dangerous places. You've deeply touched my life.

Harvest House, I'm blessed to work with a team that feels like family. Betty, Jean, and LaRae, it's been an honor to join hands with you on this project!

This is a book about women. But I can't forget the men in my life: To my husband, David, the love of my life. Our wonderful sons, DB and Michael and son-in-law, Ryan. And to Dad. You are mighty men of valor, all of you!

Contents

Introduction: What Is a Woman of Valor? 9

1. She Is a Fierce Fighter 15

2. She Makes Herself Strong 35

3. She Laughs at the Future 55

4. She Builds Her House Wisely 73

5. She Prays Hard 93

6. She Dares to Dream Big 113

7. She Leads with Kindness 133

8. She Gives Her Life Away 151

9. She Is Destined to Reign 171

   Valor Quest: Woman of Valor Study Guide 183

   Notes 219

   Bibles Referenced 223

What Is a Woman of Valor?

I believe most women, deep down inside, long to be world-changers. To use their powerful influence for good. To give life to those around them. The Bible has a beautiful term to describe this kind of woman. She is called "a woman of valor."

I've been privileged throughout my life to be influenced by many strong and courageous women. From my own mother and grand-mothers. Teachers and mentors and coaches. Church and community leaders. Extended family members. The list goes on.

Perhaps you're like me. Most of us can point to strong women who shaped our lives somewhere along the way. They left their imprint on our characters, our hopes, and our dreams. At times, they sacrificed some of their own hopes and dreams so we could realize ours.

> To educate a girl is to educate a nation.

Africans have a beautiful way of referring to all women as "mothers"—whether or not they have children, whether they are married or single. They believe all women give life to their families and communities. Africans know mothers can change the world. Thus they have this saying: "To educate a girl is to educate a nation."

By their very nature, women are life-givers. Throughout history courageous and noble women have discovered a mysterious truth: They found life when they gave their lives away—pouring themselves

out in service to their families, to their communities, and to the hurting and broken of this world. Nowhere is this more celebrated than in
the pages of Scripture.

The Bible presents us with captivating examples of courageous
women who changed their world. Some were wives and mothers. Others were prophets, judges, and leaders. Many were old and wise. Others were filled with the passion of youth. All were warriors. Life-givers.
They were women of valor. And they discovered the secret that when
they gave their lives away to others, they got far more in return.

The Hebrew term used in Proverbs 31:10 for the famed "virtuous
woman," *eshet chayil*, can be better translated "woman of valor." The
concept of a woman of valor is quite common among Jews, even today.
Here's why: A long-standing custom among Jews the evening before
Shabbat is for the husband to recite or even sing what is actually an
acrostic poem in Proverbs 31, "The Woman of Valor," to honor his wife.

Ruth is an outsider to the Jewish faith and a penniless young widow
when we're introduced to her story in the Bible. Yet she is recognized by
Boaz, her future husband—along with the entire Jewish community—
as worthy of this most honorable term, *eshet chayil* (Ruth 3:11). So
"woman of valor" can apply to women who are not wives. To women
who are not insiders. And clearly, it's not wealth, education, or social
standing that define the woman of valor. So what is it?

Simply put, *valor* is personal bravery in the face of danger, especially in battle. In its nearly 100 uses in the Old Testament, the word
for valor, *chayil*, is most often used to describe warriors, such as King
David's "mighty men" (2 Samuel). Sometimes it's used to describe God
Himself, especially when He gives power to His people to fight a battle.

I find the term *woman of valor* both compelling and poetic. My
30-something daughter, a young wife and mother, says she likes this
expression because it makes her think of courage and strength. Valor
is courage. But the woman of valor also embodies honor, strength of
character, virtue, and so much more.

I believe we need to become women of valor as we face our own battles today. Unlike the woman of Proverbs 31, we enjoy the benefits of countless breakthroughs in medicine, science, and travel. Technology has put the world at our fingertips. But consider some

> The woman of valor is essentially a warrior, a "fighter" at heart.

of the enemies confronting our world. Addiction, divorce, domestic violence, child abuse, poverty, unemployment, pornography, human trafficking, homelessness, and the general aimlessness of many of our youth loom large. Even sociologists speak in terms of the "war on poverty" or the "war on drugs." Not to mention that we're bombarded by news of one or more seemingly random terror attacks around the world on any given day. If this isn't war, my friend, I don't know what is.

The woman of valor revealed in the Bible is essentially a warrior, a "fighter" at heart. She fights not only for her personal world, but also for the world around her. As I listen to conversations with women of all ages, stages, and walks of life, I hear a recurring theme—their heart's desire to be strong for their families and communities. In short, they long to be *strong* women of God who influence the world.

How My Quest Began

My vantage point as a Christian wife and mother, and now grandmother, has shaped my perspective on what it means to be a woman. However, I used to be an agnostic with feminist leanings, so I've explored many opposing views over the years in my quest for the truth.

When I accepted Christ and then met my husband about a year after that, my thinking was challenged as I dove headlong into a study of the Word of God. I confess that I made some missteps as I tried to fit into the "perfect biblical wife" role, as many had defined it. Somehow the stereotype failed to measure up to the inner stirrings of God's call on my life. Nor did it do justice to the exciting portrayals of women I saw in the pages of Scripture. That role seemed too tame, too safe, and maybe a little self-centered. But I also knew to steer clear of the fiercely feminist interpretations of womanhood. I had already been there and found them lacking. My quest for success had finally collided with my hunger for truth.

My journey to understand biblical womanhood led me to seek God, to pray, to study His Word, and to learn from the examples of women who love and serve Him. My background in both journalism and counseling helped shape my thinking. Plus, I've been married to my husband, David, for almost four decades. David has served as senior pastor in the same church for nearly that long, and our ministry has produced relationships with a church family that now numbers in the thousands. This experience has provided the kind of rich perspective made possible only over time.

Over the years, I've been privileged to know and work alongside many strong women of valor. I'm reminded of one dear friend who, with her husband and four small children, bravely left the comforts of home to minister to unreached people groups in Asia. And the young doctor, the first in her family to go to college, who now practices medicine among the poor. Another friend grew up as a member of the untouchable class in India. She has earned her PhD, and now oversees a large organization teaching life skills and educating women and children throughout India, all the while sharing the love of Jesus.

Then there are the countless women who give their lives away quietly but powerfully as they pour life into their children at home—the impact of their work extends to generations yet to come. And let's not forget the brave warriors who care for infirm or aging loved ones. These women would all affirm the same truth I've discovered: We find life as we give our lives away.

> We find life as we give our lives away.

The woman of valor is also described as a woman of "honor" (Proverbs 31:25 NKJV). Throughout the Bible, valor and honor go hand in hand.[1] As we learn about valor, I'll also touch on several foundational insights on the subject of honor.

A fresh look at *eshet chayil*, the woman of valor, has opened my eyes to a greater understanding of the joy, fulfillment, and impact God desires for us to have on our world. It's time to reclaim this strong, brave, and beautiful portrayal of womanhood.

Let's explore what the Bible teaches about the woman of valor. We'll see that she is courageous, wise, generous, and kindhearted. She is passionate about relationships. She is both servant and leader. She's willing to take a stand. She defends the weak. She believes in miracles. She follows hard after God but also has a light heart and a sense of humor. The woman of valor is a dreamer who helps others realize their dreams, so her presence is vital to helping launch the next generation. She knows who she is and who she is not—and she knows what God has called her to do.

How to Use This Book

Lots of voices speak to women today. Some are all around us, some are in our own heads. We have no shortage of ideas about what it means to live as a "biblical woman." Maybe you're like me. You're tired of the debates. You're looking for a road map, not a progress report. I invite you on a quest to find a different path—not as a liberated or traditional woman, but as a woman of valor.

Whenever I want to hear from God, it's important to find a time and place to meet with Him each day. It also helps to have a plan. So I've prepared a "Valor Quest" study guide for you at the back of this book. I encourage you to prayerfully read each chapter before you answer the questions for that chapter in the study guide.

Your journey will probably look different from mine. I'd simply like to come alongside you as a trusted friend and help walk you through some biblical wisdom, point out some things I've learned along the way, and then turn you loose to find your own path.

I believe you'll be inspired by examples of women of valor in the Bible, along with several from history and others from all walks of life today. I'll also share stories and practical tips from some of my friends and heroes—everyday women of valor.

Let's learn from them. What are their secrets of strength and their stories of joy? How are they making a difference in their homes, their communities, and the world? How might we do the same? I hope we will discover why a woman of valor can be a powerful leader and a life-giving influence in her family and community. And why she is a world-changer.

Families today are hurting. Children lack direction. Marriages have a 50 percent fail rate. Communities grow more fragile by the day. Our culture groans. Who is this woman of valor, and what can we learn from her? Surely, we've never needed her more than now.

1

She Is a Fierce Fighter

*A woman of valour who can find? For
her price is far above rubies.*

Proverbs 31:10 JPS[1]

I was six years old at the time, and to this day I can't remember ever
being more enthralled by a Christmas-morning surprise than I was
when I opened the adorable, lifelike baby doll named Kitten. It was
love at first sight.

My brand-new doll had rosebud lips, soft blonde hair, and blue
open-and-close eyes. I was mesmerized by her gracefully crafted, soft
vinyl hands and feet. With her cuddly cloth body, she looked and felt
like a real baby. In my eyes, she was perfection. And she was mine to
love.

This exquisite baby doll, a creation of the Madame Alexander doll
company, was the doll above all dolls for little girls growing up in the
1960s. Even today, collectors treasure the classic, vintage Baby Kitten.

Right up there with Baby Kitten was another awesome gift that
year—my Mattel toy Winchester rifle. The "only toy rifle realistic enough to bear the Winchester name," touted the television

commercials. I was simply captivated by the fact that it fired real "safe-shooting plastic shells." Just what I needed to be a *real* cowboy. I guess my mom, who had grown up riding horses on a farm, and my dad, a World War II submarine veteran and a sharpshooter himself, didn't see any harm in their young daughter toting a toy rifle alongside her cherished baby doll.

I persuaded my parents to buy me a pair of PF Flyers, the sneakers that were all the rage. I lobbied for the boys' version—the high-top black kind—because the low-topped, white sneakers for girls seemed a little dull in comparison. Besides, the now-classic black high-tops promised to make you "run faster and jump higher."

> It seemed natural for me to nurture, but also to defend, protect, and sometimes fight—especially on behalf of those who couldn't fight for themselves.

So with Baby Kitten over one shoulder and my Winchester rifle on the other, I sported my new high-top PF Flyers to complete the "look." I was part nurturer and part warrior—and I played both roles with enthusiasm. There was excitement in caring for the babies, fighting the enemies, and guarding the forts we made in the woods. Even as a little girl, it seemed natural for me to nurture, but also to defend, protect, and sometimes fight—especially on behalf of those who couldn't fight for themselves.

Somewhere along the way, I decided that boys' pastimes were far more interesting than those traditionally imagined for girls. And with about a dozen boys in our neighborhood, my afternoons were easily filled with baseball, basketball, football, riding bikes, building forts, and all manner of fun. My understanding parents allowed their ten-year-old tomboy daughter the freedom to follow her thirst for adventure, though I doubt they knew she had also learned to cuss and fight like the boys.

But at around 12 or 13, I discovered that boys were much more interesting as "boyfriends." It was all rather innocent back then—going steady meant a girl would wear her boyfriend's ID bracelet or sterling-silver friendship ring. And she could expect a box of candy on Valentine's Day. Almost overnight, being a girl became much more intriguing.

By high school, my love of adventure quite naturally worked its way into the realm of sports. Back then, sports for girls usually meant cheerleading or drill team for our state championship football team. But it was now the 1970s, and all kinds of doors would soon be open to women.

Just how to navigate these nurturer-warrior themes would turn out to be something of a quest for me. Many years later I would discover these twin aspects of womanhood portrayed in the pages of the Bible. But as I grew up, the Bible was certainly not the place I looked for clues about much of anything. In fact, once I reached high school I walked away from my childhood faith. And by college I had stopped believing in God altogether.

Part Nurturer, Part Warrior

As it turned out, I would need both the nurturer and the warrior sides of my personality to handle a troubling racial incident in high school. My small town of Tucker, Georgia, a suburb of Atlanta, was typical of many small towns in the South. In Tucker, football was king. And Tucker High School consistently produced state championship teams, along with a few NFL players.

In the 1960s Tucker was also home to the national headquarters of the Ku Klux Klan. I had noticed the KKK shingle hanging from a doorway the very first time I walked down Main Street. We had just moved from Virginia, and even as an eight-year-old I was stunned by the hatred represented by that sign.

That was around the same time staunch segregationist Lester Maddox, later the governor of Georgia, refused to serve black customers in his Atlanta restaurant, Pickrick. In direct defiance of the Civil Rights Act of 1964, Maddox and some employees and customers armed themselves with ax handles and guarded the doorway of the restaurant against protesters. Ever the publicity monger, Maddox passed out small plastic ax handles throughout the city as a symbol of segregation.

I can still remember the race riots, burning, and looting that swept through Atlanta and other cities across the country that summer. Just one state over, Governor George Wallace of Alabama physically blocked the entrance of a building at the University of Alabama in an attempt to prevent two black young people from registering.

Racial tensions were still simmering when I entered high school around 1970. Our town was mostly white. Tucker High School had a student body of about 3000, with only about 20 or so African American students. That handful of black students—most of them related to one another—were all from one small, ramshackle neighborhood on a dirt road a couple of miles from the school, tucked behind the industrial section of town. For the most part, they were largely ignored at our school. Not necessarily mistreated, but practically invisible.

That is, until a young sophomore named Carolyn, nicknamed "Peaches," tried out for cheerleading and was selected for one of the 12 coveted spots on our varsity cheerleading squad.

It's safe to say that if football was king in my high school, then cheerleading was queen. For a girl to make cheerleading practically guaranteed her a higher spot on the social pecking order. But up to that time our school had never even had a black athlete, much less a black cheerleader. Carolyn was the first. It was my senior year and I was the cheerleading captain, but I'm sure I didn't fully grasp her courage as she dared to step over the color line.

Every afternoon I coached our squad through a two-hour practice in preparation for the Friday-night varsity football games. I made it a point to look out for Carolyn and help her adjust to the world of cheerleading. She was smart, an excellent athlete, and caught on quickly. But she had no transportation, so I took her home after practice.

I remember driving down the road to her house. I hadn't known it even existed although I'd passed it for years. It wasn't paved, and I wonder now if the run-down shacks scattered along that road even had electricity or plumbing.

For the most part, our first season was uneventful. But trouble had been quietly brewing with one of the parents. I will never forget that afternoon after practice. We were working hard to prepare for the all-important summer cheerleading camp—the same camp where we had been honored with the "Best All-Around Squad" award for the previous two years.

One of the cheerleaders, who was a friend of mine, pulled me aside and practically hissed these words: "My mama said she will not have her daughter rooming at camp with a n_____." And then she made a face of utter disgust at the mere thought of it.

It was all I could do to keep from slapping her, but she could tell I was breathing fire. I spit out these words with a carefully measured fury that surprised us both: "You will never, *ever* say that word again." Just about that time, Mary, a kindhearted member of our squad, quickly stepped forward and said, "Don't worry. I'll room with Carolyn."

Somehow, as I recall, it all worked out. We even came together as a top-notch cheerleading squad and won the Best All-Around Squad trophy at camp again that summer. Yet I don't know what became of Carolyn after high school, or to the handful of students who lived in her tiny neighborhood. I wish I did. I wish I knew they've all had good lives. But it was the early '70s in the Deep South, and because of long-held racial tensions and divides, despite their intelligence and abilities, life seemed to hold much less promise for them than for all the other students in my school.

And to me, as a young person who had opportunities I feared they did not, that seemed outrageously unfair.

My Quest for Biblical Womanhood

My experience that year as cheerleading captain helped me learn to embrace the nurturer and warrior roles. There were times to be gentle and times to fight. This theme of fighting against injustice would repeat itself again and again, especially in college.

I remember inviting a sharp young African American fellow journalism student to dinner at my sorority house at the University of Georgia. We were not dating, but even our work together on journalism school projects caused a stir. I was just one of the many young, idealistic college students of my day who wanted to change the world and help bring about racial reconciliation.

Sadly, I didn't associate any of these stirrings with God. And as I mentioned, by the time I got to college, I had pretty much stopped believing in God altogether. I found plenty of excuses for walking away from the faith of my childhood. For one thing, a few of the worst racists I knew were also among the churchgoing crowd. (I wrongly chose to ignore the many sincere believers on the front lines of social change.) Plus, becoming "religious" was social suicide in my particular crowd. I was sure if God existed He probably wasn't interested in my desire to make a difference in the world. How wrong I was.

Looking back, I was bound to meet Jesus sooner or later. I'll share more about that in another chapter. But some strong Christian friends were praying for me, and I am sure my parents were too. And there was the wise pastor from my family's home church who placed a book in my hands and simply said, "One day when you have some questions, read this."

About a year later, I did just that. I not only read *Mere Christianity* by former atheist and Oxford scholar C.S. Lewis, but I was thoroughly convicted. I realized that for all my good intentions, I had lived a completely self-centered life. I put the book down and gave my heart and soul to Jesus Christ.

Right away, my friends noticed the change. Not surprising, since they had known me only as an agnostic with somewhat feminist leanings. And when a young seminary student named David Chadwick came knocking on my door the following summer for our blind date, I found myself falling in love…and heading in a direction that would surely be a 180-degree shift from my original plans for my life. Or so I thought.

About the same time, I had entered the corporate world, landing a dream job with one of the top companies in Atlanta. They had recruited me for practically my entire senior year of college. I was brought on board as one of the very first women selected for upper-level management. But I found myself uninspired by life on the fast track, and I wasn't motivated by the hefty salary. I failed to see what difference I could make in the world of high-powered corporate work.

I continued the quest to understand my life's calling, now curious about what it meant to be a Christian woman. David and I began talking about marriage. We made plans to move to Houston, where he would complete his doctoral internship in a vibrant downtown church. My company was more than generous and offered to give me a leave of absence—the position, they assured me, would be waiting when I came back to Atlanta 15 months later. I never returned to that position.

> One of the first things I noticed after I accepted Jesus is that the Bible made sense.

David and I got married and moved to Texas. I jumped into my new role as a pastor's wife and discovered that I thrived on our ministry together with young married couples. My faith was still brand-new and very exciting to me. I began to study the Bible in earnest, eager to understand what it meant to be a believer.

One of the first things I noticed after I accepted Jesus is that the Bible made sense. I had tried to read it before I surrendered my life to the Lord and found it completely confusing. But now I could understand the words—as if there was an "interpreter" in my head. I fully embraced the strong messages I found in the Bible about the importance of marriage and the family. Quite surprisingly, I also grew to appreciate the role of the husband as the spiritual head of his family. I'll talk in more detail about that in chapter 4.

At that time, however, much of the teaching in the 1970s defined biblical womanhood almost exclusively in terms of a woman's family and homemaking skills, with little attention given to her calling to serve the Lord. This imbalance, I believe, was a reaction to the aggressive feminist dogma of the day that undermined the vital role of the family.

During my agnostic years, I had already explored the feminist view of womanhood and found it unsatisfying, so I was ready to embrace a strong, biblical message about marriage and the family. I wanted to follow Christ wholeheartedly, whatever that looked like. But without realizing it, I tried to squeeze myself into a mold that didn't fit with who God had made me to be. In trying to become the "perfect biblical wife," as some had defined her, I sometimes got so absorbed with managing a home and honing my decorating skills that I forgot about pouring my life out on behalf of the hurting and broken.

Over time, as I grew in my relationship with the Lord, I began to understand the richness and freedom of womanhood as God created it. It was all right there in the pages of Scripture. I discovered challenging and exciting stories. Women in the Bible fought battles, overturned genocidal plots, gave birth to world-changing children, raised strong families, and suffered and died for their faith.

> Our priority should be Jesus and His calling on our lives—wherever that takes us.

And it seemed to me that the modern Christian woman had become a little too safe and sanitized—she was the nurturer without the warrior.

One friend, who had raised her children at great risk on the mission field in Africa, challenged me with her observation about the

American church. She thought it sometimes overemphasized the family—as important as family is—to the exclusion of mission. Our priority should not be to focus on the family, she commented. "It should be to focus on Jesus and His calling on our lives—wherever that takes us."

Another Look at the Proverbs 31 Woman

More recently, I decided to take a fresh look at the famed Proverbs 31 woman when David and I were working on companion books on marriage, one for husbands and one for wives.[2]

The Bible tells us she was a "virtuous" woman, clothed with strength and honor (verse 25 NKJV). Since I was writing about the subject of honor at the time, I was curious to find out why the Proverbs 31 woman is described as honorable. And what made her strong? I began to dig a little deeper into the Bible passage describing this unnamed character.

Now, I confess that Proverbs 31—with its lengthy tribute to the celebrated virtuous woman—had become a tired, overworked passage of Scripture for me. Or maybe it just made me feel tired and overworked to read about her. Regrettably, the account of this remarkable woman morphed, over the centuries, into a sort of "to-do" list. A job description for the Christian woman that left many feeling inadequate and more than a little exhausted.

Honestly, who can be an amazing wife, mother, and homemaker, and run several businesses, serve the poor, and be honored in her city all at the same time? Additionally, some of the commentaries on the Proverbs 31 woman emphasized only her role as nurturer and manager of her home and family. They seemed to leave out her warrior side altogether.

Rediscovering the Woman of Valor

I was quite surprised to discover that in the Orthodox Jewish Bible, the virtuous woman of Proverbs 31 is called a "woman of valor." Turns out "woman of valor" is a better translation of the Hebrew term *eshet chayil*, which is found in verse 10 and more commonly referred to as a "virtuous woman."

Woman of valor. What a beautiful description. Why had I never heard this term spoken in Christian circles? I learned that "woman of valor" is often used among Jews and Messianic Jews even today. Every Friday evening before Shabbat, the husband will recite or sing the poem "A Woman of Valor" to honor his wife—to reflect upon and be thankful for all she has done for him, their family, and for the community throughout the past week.

A quick search of the internet yielded dozens of references to the "woman of valor" among Jews and Messianic Jews the world over. There were "Women of Valor" poems, plaques, websites, books—even Women of Valor conferences.

Valor Defined

So I was curious. Exactly what is *valor*? Simple dictionary definitions of the word *valor* convey the idea of courage and bravery, especially in battle. The word can also imply that a person of valor possesses special skill or accomplishment.

But the biblical definition for valor, or *chayil*, is much more vibrant and rich with meaning. It includes concepts like courage, strength, honor, and even wealth. As defined in a Hebrew word dictionary, *chayil* means "strength, bravery, capability, skill, valor, wealth, troop, army, warrior."[3] In its nearly 100 uses in the Old Testament, *valor* or *chayil* is most often used in a military sense. It's the same word used to describe King David's "mighty men of valor" (1 Chronicles 12:21 ESV). Or God, as a warrior for His people. I learned that *chayil* is the same word for heaven's angel armies.

> Valor, or *chayil*, is vibrant and rich with meaning. It includes concepts like courage, strength, honor, and even wealth.

A Warrior Emphasis

Imagine my joy at learning that the Proverbs 31 woman is a warrior. Part nurturer and part warrior. The twin themes of nurturer and warrior were right there in the text! In the process of learning about the woman of valor, I found a new hero and the inspiration for this book.

Why, you might ask, would the Bible use a military term like *valor* to describe the ordinary woman in Proverbs 31? No doubt she is quite capable. She encourages and supports her husband, she raises successful kids, she manages a thriving home, and she runs a successful business. She serves the poor. And in that day her "household" probably included extended family members, a few servants, and maybe some livestock. So if you're feeling overwhelmed with your own to-do list, take heart. This woman understood the challenges of multitasking.

But again, why a military term? It would seem more realistic to look at her as the "capable" or "competent" wife, or the "virtuous woman," as she is called in various Bible translations.

It helps to remember that life for the Proverbs 31 woman of valor in the Bible included facing deadly plagues; marauding thieves and armies; extreme heat, cold, and hunger; and all manner of pestilence. Daily she faced threats from without and within. She needed to be strong, brave, and always alert. She certainly needed to be a "woman of valor," because in one way or another, she was always at war.

But on a spiritual level, doesn't it make sense to realize that every woman, every home, and every community, in every part of the world is also at war today? As long as we are members of God's kingdom here on earth, we live in enemy-occupied territory. The Bible is full of warnings for all believers to be on the alert, watchful, armed, and ready for battle against the enemy of our souls. It makes me wonder why we lost sight of such an important concept as the woman of valor in the first place. We'll explore the answer to that question in chapter 2.

What if the devil, who has hated women from day one,[4] has been intent upon robbing the woman of valor of her true meaning, purpose, and worth, as God designed her? Let's face it. If you defeat the woman, you can attack marriage, families, and communities. My friend Barbara, who ministered in the inner city, once said it this way: "If you take down the mamas, you will take down the babies." I hope you'll agree. It's time to reclaim the woman of valor.

Everyday Women of Valor

My understanding what it means to become a woman of valor has also been shaped by what I've observed firsthand in nearly four decades of ministry. I've watched ordinary women pouring their lives out in extraordinary service to the Lord.

David and I have had the privilege of working alongside ministry partners in various places in the world, and many of those partners have been everyday women of valor in all walks of life: wives, mothers, teachers, missionaries, counselors, doctors, government leaders, relief workers. We have seen how God works out His purpose and pours His strength into women who are called to give their lives to the hurting and broken. Sometimes this happens in the most surprising and unexpected of places.

Barbara's Story: A Tough and Tender Warrior

One of the most inspiring "real-life" women of valor I have ever known was Barbara Brewton Cameron. This vibrant and joyful woman with an easy laugh and a giant heart was also a powerful leader in her community. She became a dear friend, mentor, and role model. Barbara was in her mid-sixties when she died suddenly of a stroke several years ago. During our 15-year friendship, Barbara opened my eyes to the powerful impact one ordinary woman can have on her family, her community, and an entire city.

Years before I met Barbara, her husband had been gunned down in a drive-by shooting while walking home from work, leaving her with three small children to raise on her own. "He was a wonderful man—a good husband and father—and I was devastated," she said. "I didn't even want to go on living."

The Double Oaks community in Charlotte where Barbara lived was described by the *New York Times* as one of the most violent neighborhoods in America. News reports dubbed it "an open-air drug market of heroin and cocaine." Gunfire was common around the small, graffiti-marked houses. The community also had one of the highest murder rates in the country.

After her husband's murder, Barbara fled to a safer neighborhood to raise her children. But God began to pursue her, and several years later she accepted Christ into her life. "I began to hear His voice," she said. "I knew there was a far greater plan that God had for me.

"God told me to go back to the old neighborhood and rescue the children. And so I did." Barbara said the Lord spoke to her through Matthew 25:35-36: "I was hungry and you gave Me food; I was thirsty and you gave Me drink; I was a stranger and you took Me in; I was naked and you clothed Me; I was sick and you visited Me; I was in prison and you came to Me" (NKJV). She sensed God calling to her through the words of Scripture: "Inasmuch as you did it to one of the least of these My brethren, you did it to Me" (v. 40 NKJV).

Barbara was affectionately referred to throughout her community as "Pastor Cameron." I got to know Barbara when our church formed a partnership with her ministry. She created relationships with area churches like ours, as well as city services and local food banks.

Barbara understood firsthand the hopeless despair faced by her community. "I thought of the single moms who were being used and abused by drug dealers," she added. "And I thought about the babies." To Barbara, all children were "babies."

"A while back, the men were taken from this community by gangs, drugs, and alcohol," she explained. "But as long as the moms were at home, there was hope for the children."

"When crack cocaine got the mamas," she added, "then the babies were at the mercy of every kind of evil."

It was those children Barbara was going back to rescue. She found a small, dilapidated house to rent in the neighborhood and turned it into a mission home to care for children each afternoon. "I gave the little ones baths and helped the older ones with homework. I'd feed them, too, since they were always hungry. Sometimes I would just fix hotdogs. The mamas were not watching out for their babies, so I had to step in and take care of them."

Barbara found volunteers to help her and collaborated with other churches. In time her ministry grew and she became known as the woman who defied drugs and gangs to clean up one of Charlotte's most dangerous neighborhoods.

Not everyone was happy with Barbara's return to Double Oaks. The drug dealers who controlled the neighborhood began issuing threats. She lobbied for a greater police presence in the community. She worked with the Charlotte-Mecklenburg Housing Partnership, Habitat for Humanity, and others to buy run-down houses from slumlords and get these homes into the hands of neighborhood owners.

Years later, a former hit man told Barbara he had been hired by a Charlotte drug dealer to kill her because she was hurting business. He would sit outside the open window listening to her preach the gospel. After seeing her, something inside would not let him carry out the hit. Later, Barbara told me, the man accepted Jesus.

Imperceptibly at first, Double Oaks began to change. Barbara bought property nearby, where she opened Community Outreach Christian Ministries. In a short time, Community Outreach outgrew its building.

About the same time, our own church, Forest Hill, was also in need of a building to accommodate our growth. But one night at a council meeting, David and our elders sensed God saying to them, "Build Community Outreach a new church before you build your own." So we had a three-year campaign called "Brick by Brick." Forest Hill Church members gave sacrificially to help Community Outreach build a brand-new church— a church that continued to expand the impact of the gospel throughout the community. Barbara received national acclaim for the work she did fighting crime in the Double Oaks community. City officials even renamed the area Genesis Park, symbolic of its new beginning.

> God can do mighty things through one ordinary woman of valor.

When Barbara died in 2008, her family asked David to officiate the funeral. Our church was filled to capacity with members of both African American and white churches from all over the city. Pastor Cameron is remembered as the Mother Teresa of Genesis Park. The once-forgotten community is an example of how God can do mighty things through one ordinary woman of valor.

What Takes the Fight Out of a Woman?

If we want our families and communities to thrive, we must reclaim what it means to be women of valor. We are challenged to become tenderhearted warriors like my friend Barbara.

I've come to believe we women are at our best when engaged in a fight for someone outside ourselves. When giving our lives away. Most women I know have both nurturer and warrior in their nature. No matter how gentle the exterior, the fierce fighter comes out when protecting someone we love, defending the weak, or chasing a dream.

> I've come to believe we women are at our best when engaged in a fight for someone outside ourselves.

I'm reminded of my friend Jacqui, who has been waging a long and agonizing fight to gain custody of the daughter she has lovingly fostered. Jacqui put it well when she vowed, "I will not give up. After all, I'm a 'Mama Bear' fighting for her cub." Or our daughter, Bethany, a young mom with four little ones under six who somehow educates her children at home, manages nighttime feedings, and juggles the busy life of a pastor's wife. There's Jessie, our daughter-in-law, who recently climbed Mount Kilimanjaro to help raise support for a ministry that makes childbirth safer for women in Ethiopia.

Or Kristi, who heads up a college scholarship fund for young people with big dreams but few resources. She mentors and coaches these talented dreamers, constantly providing a "mother bear" kind of wisdom and love.

Yes, most women know what I'm talking about when I speak of their fierce, fighter side. It's no wonder so many of us believe deep within that we can change the world. And tucked within the pages of Scripture, we perhaps have some clues as to how and why God designed us as both nurturers and warriors.

If I wanted to wreck families and cripple a culture, I would simply take the fight out of a woman. And how does one do that?

For one thing, you crush her dreams, again and again, beginning when she is a child. Criticize her daily and rob her of her sense of worth. Make her feel unloved, or unaccepted, or unsafe. Tell her she'll never measure up to the standard of beauty or achievement she sees all around her. Nothing she does is ever good enough. Convince her Facebook images are real. And above all, persuade her that God is never satisfied by who she is or what she does.

Or come at it from an altogether different angle. Entice her to follow the success and money trail. Make her think life is all about her—her beauty, her brains, her body. Her bank account. Her personal best. Suddenly life is all about being the "best in show." She becomes a specimen to be admired. Worshiped. Adored. But never truly loved or cherished. Convince her to be self-serving instead of self-giving. To become consumed with taking life instead of giving life. Tell her caring for a husband and launching children makes her "less than."

Either way works. Whether you beat her down or inflate her ego, the woman becomes self-absorbed—the center of her world. This turns her into a wrecking ball instead of a world-changer. Then numb her with addictions and idols so she can't feel the pain…until it's too late. Above all, convince her this path must be traveled alone.

Ready for War

That's why, if a woman truly wants to become a woman of valor who can change her world, she must first be convinced of the need to fight. She must fight the right fight with the right weapons. She must learn how to draw her strength from the Lord. In short, to become a woman of valor, she must first prepare for war.

Over the years I've seen women lose too many battles—against low self-esteem, anxiety, addiction, bitterness, unbelief. Battles for their marriages and children. Stress fractures from the modern life can leave a woman weak and broken, unable or unwilling to fight for herself and for those she loves.

But I am convinced it doesn't have to be this way. Our battles can be won if we're more alert to the Enemy's tactics and if we are intentional to not only build our faith but also to guard it. God has created us as both nurturers and warriors. And when our identity is firmly anchored in our relationship with Christ, we have everything we need to be victorious. Our Commander in Chief has given us His Holy Spirit to empower our prayers, His Word as our weapon, and a community of faith to back us up.

Let's face it. Women are always at war of one kind or another. We face the obvious battles that rage all around us. Plus, we wrestle against forces that attack us from within. The Bible reminds us that, at their root, all these various battles have a spiritual source—our Enemy, the devil, and his forces of darkness. Thus our strategy must begin in the spiritual realm.

> What would happen if, together, we became an army of women? Women of valor. Armed and dangerous to the devil.

That's why I want to encourage you to take your time as you prayerfully go through this book. You may need to create some white space in your life to allow God to speak to your heart. The "Valor Quest" study guide in the back is designed to help you explore what God might be saying. What would happen if, together, we became an army of women? Women of valor. Armed and dangerous to the devil. Women who are ready for war.

The Bible promises that if we submit to God and resist the devil, he will flee (James 4:7). That smells like victory to me. It's time for us, as women of valor, to take our place as part of God's special forces. The world groans, our communities are crumbling, and our families cry out for us to rise up and fight. Evil may be evil, but the war against evil is good. It's worth our best effort. Let's explore some ways a woman of valor can begin now to rise up and make herself strong.

A Woman of Valor

A Woman of Valor, who can find? She is more precious than corals.

Her husband places his trust in her and profits only thereby.

She brings him good, not harm, all the days of her life.

She seeks out wool and flax and cheerfully does the work of her hands. She is like the trading ships, bringing food from afar.

She gets up while it is still night to provide food for her household, and a fair share for her staff. She considers a field and purchases it, and plants a vineyard with the fruit of her labors.

She invests herself with strength and makes her arms powerful.

She senses that her trade is profitable; her light does not go out at night.

She stretches out her hands to the distaff and her palms hold the spindle.

She opens her hands to the poor and reaches out her
    hands to the needy.
She has no fear of the snow for her household, for all her
    household is dressed in fine clothing.
She makes her own bedspreads; her clothing is of fine
    linen and luxurious cloth.
Her husband is known at the gates, where he sits with
    the elders of the land.
She makes and sells linens; she supplies the merchants
    with sashes.
She is robed in strength and dignity, and she smiles at
    the future.
She opens her mouth with wisdom and a lesson of kind-
    ness is on her tongue.
She looks after the conduct of her household and never
    tastes the bread of laziness.
Her children rise up and make her happy; her husband
    praises her:
"Many women have excelled, but you excel them all!"
Grace is elusive and beauty is vain, but a woman who
    fears God—she shall be praised.
Give her credit for the fruit of her labors, and let her
    achievements praise her at the gates.[5]

2

She Makes Herself Strong

She equips herself with strength [spiritual, mental, and physical fitness for her God-given task] and makes her arms strong.

PROVERBS 31:17 AMP

When you get right down to it, being a woman of valor is not just about courage or strength. It also has a lot to do with love, because love is what makes us brave. Most every good woman I know would gladly lay down her life for those she loves. I can still remember when the nurse placed our first newborn baby in my arms. Suddenly I was a mama bear, and I was absolutely certain that if it came down to it, I would defend this child to the death.

That's the kind of fierce love God has poured into us as women. It's the same love that motivates us to become fighters. Remember, God created us to be both nurturers and warriors.

> Love makes us brave.

But I'll say it again. We are losing wars we should be winning. Wars for our marriages and our children. Wars to reclaim our communities. Wars against strongholds and addictions. Dear friend, we must win our own battles at home if we want to win battles on behalf of the lost, the sick, and the broken. To wage war as women of valor, we must be well prepared. We must be loving. And we must become incredibly, powerfully strong.

We've learned that the two Hebrew words used to describe the Proverbs 31 woman, *eshet chayil,* are best translated "woman of valor" (verse 10). She's not only loving and courageous; she is strong. "Strength and honour are her clothing" (verse 25 KJV). And "she dresses herself with strength and makes her arms strong" (verse 17 ESV).

Ultimately, we'll see that the real source of her strength is her relationship with the Lord—we'll talk more about that later. But for now, let's consider the obvious: This woman had to be *physically* strong to face the challenges of her day. She "works with eager hands…gets up while it is still night;" provides food and jobs for her family and servants; buys a field… "plants a vineyard"…and "sets about her work vigorously" (verses 13,15-16). Even her arms, we're told, "are strong for her tasks" (verse 17). Another version reads, "She…makes her arms strong" (ESV). I get tired just reading about her.

But I have to smile when I think about her "strong arms" because it reminds me of a conversation I had with my friend and prayer partner, Beth. We have both loved being mothers and now love being grandmothers. But the physical demands that come with raising children are a challenge for any mother. There's the continual lifting, dressing, bathing, and feeding of little ones, not to mention the process of labor and delivery just to get them here. I'm reminded of a war movie I saw years ago. A female fighter pilot is injured. When asked by her comrade if she is okay, she shoots back, "Look, I gave birth to a nine-pound baby. I think I can handle it!" I can totally relate, since each of my three babies checked in weighing over nine pounds.

Beth and I would agree that when we raised our own children, we picked them up so often that our arms (and our backs) grew strong. Beth's babies were also large—all five sons went on to become strapping football players. But lifting grandchildren seems a little harder for us both, and Beth started doing 100 push-ups a day.

"I want to be able to lift all those grandbabies," she said, laughing. She assured me it isn't that hard. She does her first set of push-ups during her normal exercise time, and then she drops to the floor for a few more throughout the day. "It's amazing how they add up," she said.

It sounded daunting, but being a woman who loves a plan, I was inspired to give it a try. I'm nowhere near the 100 mark, but Beth assures me that if I stick with it, it's doable. Beth and her 100 daily push-ups give us a good mental picture of what it looks like to "make our arms strong."

The Amplified Bible describes the woman of valor's strength in more detail: "She equips herself with strength [spiritual, mental, and physical fitness for her God-given task] and makes her arms strong" (Proverbs 31:17 AMP). We'll talk further about practical ways to become strong. But you can begin now to think about ways to strengthen yourself in each of those three areas—spiritual, mental, and physical. Who knows? Maybe you'll even want to try Beth's 100 push-ups challenge.

Strong from the Start

We'll continue our quest to learn more about the woman of valor, created by God to be both a nurturer and a warrior. But let's pause to consider this: Have you ever thought about how God designed women from the very beginning?

Several portions of Scripture will enliven our understanding of the courage and strength God gave us. It also helps to take a look at what theologians refer to as "original intent." In other words, what did things look like before the Fall?

The Bible tell us God looked at Adam and said, "It is not good for the man to be alone" (Genesis 2:18). There was no "helper suitable" (verse 18) for Adam, so God created woman, a "helper," for the man (verse 20).

> Just like *woman of valor,* the word *helper* is a military term.

The word *helper* has been watered down over the years. Today, it can mean just about anything, from someone who lends a hand to a domestic servant. But in Hebrew, the word *ezer,* translated "helper," is quite strong. Just like *woman of valor,* the word *helper* is actually a military term. It means "to support" and comes from two words that mean "to rescue or save" and "to be strong." It's related to the word for rock, so you get a mental picture of being "strong like a rock" for those we love. To be a "helper" can also mean to watch or guard someone. So *ezer* is like an advance warning system—the wife and mother is sensitive to her family's enemies.

My husband, David, tells me he appreciates this aspect of *ezer.* Over the years, I've occasionally warned him about potentially troublesome people or situations. Perhaps you, too, seem to just "know in your knower" when something isn't quite right.

Ezer is used more than 20 times in the Old Testament, only twice referring to the woman. The rest of the time *ezer* refers to God as the one doing the helping—most often giving strength to His people during battle. God is referred to as Israel's *ezer,* their helper who gives power to His people: "The LORD is with me; he is my helper. I look in triumph on my enemies" (Psalm 118:7).

> Her fierce love can make even the most timid woman do courageous things.

I hope you see how the concept of a helper, or *ezer,* goes hand in hand with *eshet chayil,* the woman of valor. Both terms have something of a warrior flavor. Both convey the idea of protecting, nurturing, and giving support.

Her fierce love can make even the most timid woman do courageous things. Whether you're single or married, with children of your own or loving other children, my guess is you've discovered the courage and strength that rise up when you fight for someone you love.

God has created us as *ezers* who support those we love, always ready to strengthen, protect, and encourage those around us. As we continue to reflect further on our calling to be women of valor, let's keep in mind that blend of nurturer and warrior that was God's design for us. Right from the start, He created us strong.

Woman of Valor: Missing in Action

As I've shared, it was only recently that I stumbled onto the term "woman of valor" while taking a fresh look at the Proverbs 31 woman. This beautiful term has largely been lost in Christian circles. Maybe you're as curious as I am to find out how we lost sight of the "woman of valor." When did she go missing in action?

Since *eshet chayil* is a Hebrew term, we can find some answers by looking at the Proverbs 31 woman from a Jewish perspective. In case you'd like to dig a little deeper, here's what I discovered when I began to explore the woman of valor through "Hebrew eyes."

A Jewish View of the Woman of Valor

The Orthodox Jewish Bible is the only modern Bible version to translate the Hebrew words in Proverbs 31:10, *eshet chayil*, as "woman of valor." This is exactly how Jews have interpreted *eshet chayil* for centuries. That's why Jewish husbands the world over have a long-standing tradition of honoring their wives by reading or singing "A Woman of Valor" every Friday night before Shabbat.

Most Christians know the Proverbs 31 woman only as the traditional "virtuous woman" (Proverbs 31:10 KJV). Even modern translations miss the Hebrew emphasis and describe her as "excellent," "worthy," "capable," or "accomplished." These are desirable traits to describe a godly woman, but they leave out those aspects of *eshet chayil*, or "woman of valor," that convey strength or bravery.

To translate *eshet chayil* as "virtuous woman" instead of "woman of valor" opens the door to a far less powerful portrayal of our Proverbs 31 woman. Some scholars believe this to be an intentional move by Bible translators to impose their concept of biblical womanhood on the text.[1] But I'm not convinced the use of "virtuous woman" instead of "woman of valor" is simply a result of gender bias.

What's in a Word?

For one thing, words and their meanings are always changing. Some lose their original meaning, and some drop out of sight altogether. As an example, just the other day our six-year-old granddaughter was curious about some old books I was cleaning out of a closet, ready to discard. "What's that?" she said, pointing to one of them. "Oh, that's a phone book," I answered. To which she replied, "What's a phone book?" So you see, words sometimes lose their meaning because things are *always* changing. You get the point.

Over the centuries, the word *virtue* (and the word *virtuous*) evolved to mean something quite different from when it was first used. Originally, virtue was closely connected to the ideals of courage and strength. It was considered a "knightly" depiction of courage and bravery, along with moral excellence.

> Virtue without valor—or morality without courage— is too tame to fight the spiritual battles we face.

Virtue, as we know it today, generally describes goodness and moral excellence. But it has pretty much lost the ideals of strength or courage. That's why I had never considered a connection between virtue and courage until I stumbled upon the concept of the woman of valor.

Maybe that's part of the reason we've lost our appreciation of the woman as both nurturer and warrior. I've come to believe that to possess one attribute without the other can leave a woman, her family, and her entire community vulnerable. Virtue without valor—or morality without courage—is too tame to fight the spiritual battles we all face as believers. Or to live a large life for God.

Woman of Valor or Virtuous Woman?

I've heard it said that it's wise to move forward in life while at the same time glancing back at the lessons of the past. A Hebrew perspective would describe it this way: We're in a boat—rowing backward into the future—yet always looking at where we've come from. My African friends have a unique way of capturing this concept with the Swahili word *sankofa*. It means we reflect on the past to protect the future. We may even need to reclaim a lesson from the past before moving forward. Said another way, "It is not taboo to go back and fetch what we forgot."

Let's backtrack—*sankofa* style—to help us further understand the woman of valor. How can we reclaim this beautiful portrayal of the biblical woman? Is it possible to go back and fetch what we forgot? As we continue our quest, let's step back in time to search for some answers.

Lessons from the Past

To begin with, I've wondered how *eshet chayil* came to be translated as "virtuous woman" in the first place. Here's what I've learned. In Middle English the word *virtue* was derived from the Latin word *vir,* for male. It's also where we get the word *virile*. When *virtue* was first used in the 1300s, it generally meant "strength, manliness, and power, along with strong moral character."[2] The word *valor* didn't appear in common use until around the 1400s. So you see, the word *virtue*, which actually predates the word *valor*, was originally a very strong word. As I mentioned earlier, it gradually took on a meaning that all but ignored the aspects of courage and strength.

In digging around a little, I discovered that the Wycliffe Bible, handwritten by John Wycliffe in 1382, translates *chayil* as "virtue" more than 300 times. He used the word *virtue* to describe everything from military might, courage, and strength, to wealth, moral goodness, and even miracle-working power.

Wycliffe, an Oxford professor, theologian, and reformer, believed the common man should have the Bible in his everyday language. It's clear from Wycliffe's translation that *virtue*, in the common speech of the 1300s, implied strength, courage—even power—along with morality. One example of how Wycliffe translated *chayil* as "virtue" can be found in Psalm 18:39: "And thou hast girded me with virtue to battle..." (wyc). Other versions translate the *chayil* in that same verse as "strength": "You armed me with strength for battle" (Psalm 18:39).

Now back to the Proverbs 31 woman. Wycliffe translated *eshet chayil* as "strong woman": "Who shall find a strong woman?" (verse 10 wyc). Remember, the word *valor* wasn't used much until the next century. But Wycliffe's "strong woman" still captured some of the original intensity of *eshet chayil.*

How Virtue Lost Its Valor

Fast-forward two centuries to England and the King James Bible translated in the early 1600s. By this time, *eshet chayil* was translated "virtuous woman" (verse 10 kjv). As we've learned, the word *virtuous* had gradually come to mean "morally excellent, upright, or chaste," with nothing of the earlier flavor of strength or courage found in the original Hebrew. And by the late 1500s, *virtuous*, especially when describing a woman in everyday speech, meant simply "chastity, sexual purity."[3]

What's more, the word *virtue* was no longer commonly used to describe courage or strength for men. Whereas Wycliffe used the word *virtue* 327 times in his Bible translation, the King James Version uses *virtue* only six times—all of those in the New Testament, and mostly to mean excellent moral character.[4] Over the centuries, the warrior aspect of the word *virtue* seems to have disappeared altogether.

Throughout the Old Testament, the King James Version translators rendered *chayil* as "valor," most often referring to "men of valor" in a warrior context. But again, each of the three times *eshet chayil* was used to describe a woman, the translators used the term "virtuous woman" rather than "woman of valor."

> Women, families, and communities lose out when we separate virtue from valor.

In summary, we see that by the early 1600s the word *virtuous* had kept part of the word *valor's* earlier meaning of moral goodness and chastity, but had lost the connotation of strength or bravery. To emphasize it again, I believe that women, families, and communities lose out when we separate virtue from valor. Or ignore moral goodness as a life-giving aspect of courage.

Women at War

The woman of valor has gradually disappeared from Christian conversation. So why has she remained a constant presence in Jewish life? How has she endured centuries of change? For one thing, the woman of valor never left the realm of the Jewish family. Husbands continue to read or sing the song to their wives every Friday night before Shabbat. The woman of valor is a permanent fixture in Jewish thought, in the Hebrew Bible, and in the family.

Perhaps the woman of valor never left her place because the Jews have repeatedly been forced to be a people of war. Persecuted, maligned, and nearly exterminated at various points in history, the Jews have, of necessity, been constantly in a warrior mode. Maybe they

> The woman of valor defends and protects, as well as loves and nurtures.

held on to the concept of the woman of valor because they needed her strength and zeal as well as her loving, nurturing touch at home. Jewish women have been appreciated as both nurturers and warriors. Even in her family, the woman of valor defends and protects, as well as loves and nurtures.

Women throughout the Old Testament were also enduring in nature. It's easy to think of women of valor throughout the Bible who inspired me during my own spiritual journey. When I was going through years of infertility, fighting my own fight of faith, I drew strength from the example of Sarah, the wife of Abraham. Sarah was barren, but she fiercely held on to her faith despite countless setbacks and rejoiced when she and Abraham finally had Isaac in their old age.

Or there was Moses's mother, who bravely defied the king's edict to destroy all the male Hebrew babies in Egypt. She risked her life to save her son, the same son who was raised in the courts of Pharaoh and became the deliverer of God's people.

And let's not forget seven-year-old Miriam, Moses's big sister. After Moses's mother left him in a basket by the riverbank, this spunky young woman of valor went boldly up to Pharaoh's daughter, after she found the baby Moses, and offered to find a Hebrew woman to nurse the baby. Pharaoh's daughter agreed and unwittingly hired Moses's mother to nurse her own baby (Exodus 2).

Many years later, after another lengthy exile for the Jews, we find God working in the life of an orphaned teenager named Esther, an ordinary girl who dared to step out and obey God. She risked her life and saved a nation.

How Esther Saved a Nation

Sometimes I think we underestimate the power of a young person who loves God. Our choices have tremendous power for good or evil in the formative years. I confess that the story of Esther is perhaps my all-time favorite in the Old Testament. I remind you that I was the girl who walked away from God at age 15. Yet at about that same age, this young woman of valor risked her life to save her people.

It's true; God's people owe their very existence to a young Hebrew girl. God chose to work out His plan of deliverance for Israel through the courageous actions of an ordinary teenager.

Esther's story didn't start out pretty. The Jews had been taken from Jerusalem into captivity years earlier by Nebuchadnezzar, king of Babylon (Esther 2:5-7). Babylon was then defeated by Persia. When we first meet Esther, she's among the Jews living in the Persian Empire. They were a displaced people longing for home.

Esther was raised by an older, male cousin named Mordecai. Described as "lovely in form and features," her name had been changed from her original Hebrew name, Hadassah, to the Persian name Esther, or "star." Scholars believe it was connected to the Babylonian goddess Ishtar.

Even today, when a people group is captured, the conquering nation often strips away every form of national identity. I saw this firsthand during a mission trip to South Sudan prior to its independence in 2011. Throughout the 20 years of civil war, the Arab Islamic government in the north had attempted the genocidal extinction of black African Christians in southern Sudan.

Roughly two million people died and millions more were displaced. One of the North's many dehumanizing practices was to strip South Sudanese children of their Christian identity by giving them Arabic names. They were forced to attend schools where they learned to speak and read only in Arabic. Like the Jews of Esther's time, this was part of a targeted attempt to erase both their heritage and religion.

Esther was around 14 when her story began. Life as a Jew in exile was all she'd ever known. That is, until she became the queen of Persia. This startling turn of events happened after King Xerxes of Persia banished his previous queen, Vashti, for embarrassing him in public. The king's advisors came up with a plan to bring beautiful young women from every province in the Persian Empire to the king's palace. The young women were to undergo one year of the finest cosmetic treatments of that day in preparation to meet the king. He would then select his favorite candidate to be the new queen. Sounds like a modern-day reality show, doesn't it?

During her year of preparation, Esther won the favor and respect of all who knew her. The king was so impressed with Esther's beauty and grace that he selected her to be his new queen. What the king did not know was that Esther was a Jew.

Esther kept her Jewish identity a secret and remained steadfast in her allegiance to Mordecai and her people. We see her character and humility through her obedience and loyalty to Mordecai, the man who had stepped in to raise her as a surrogate father.

In time, a sinister adversary rose up from an unexpected corner. Haman, the king's highest-ranking official, despised both Mordecai and the Jewish people. He manipulated the king into signing an edict to slaughter every Jew in the Persian Empire, which at the time stretched from India to Ethiopia. This move would wipe virtually every Jew from the face of the earth.

When Mordecai learned of Haman's genocidal plot, he pleaded with Esther to beg for mercy from the king. By this time, Esther had been queen for several years and was around 20 years old. Life as queen was no doubt more comfortable than life as an exile. But she had never lost touch with Mordecai or her people.

Secrets of Strength

Esther was devastated by the news of the king's edict to destroy the Jews. But she was even more terrified by Mordecai's request. The risk for Esther was huge. Everyone throughout the palace courts knew the rule: If someone went to the king without being summoned, it was an automatic death penalty—that is, unless the king extended his golden scepter. It had been 30 days since Esther had last been summoned to appear before the king. Mordecai challenged Esther with these words: "Who knows but that you have come to your royal position for such a time as this?" (Esther 4:14).

Esther finds strength from the same place she must have always found it—from the Lord. She told Mordecai to have all the Jews gather for three days of fasting. She and her maids would do the same. When this was done, she assured him, "I will go to the king, even though it is against the law" (verse 16). Then she uttered words that are among the most stirring declarations in the entire Bible: "And if I perish, I perish" (verse 16).

At that point, I believe Esther broke the back of the adversary. The fasting and prayer then set the stage for a miraculous and strategic series of events that brought about the salvation of an entire nation. Through her courageous faith, wisdom, and ingenuity, she exposed Haman's wicked plot. The enraged king sent Haman to the very gallows he had built to hang Mordecai.

Esther proved herself to be a woman of valor. Touching briefly on our earlier discussion of Genesis 2, we also catch a glimpse of Esther as a helper, the *ezer* who warned her husband of a dangerous enemy.

The story of Esther is thrilling and full of suspense. Good triumphs over evil. And in the end, Esther influenced her husband, a pagan king, to deliver the Jews. The king promoted Mordecai to second in command in all the Persian Empire. Esther ruled as queen. And once again, we see that when one ordinary woman seeks and obeys God, extraordinary things can happen. A teenager becomes a woman of valor who dared to step out and obey God. She risked her life, and in turn, saved a nation. Let's take a closer look to find out what Esther did to make herself strong.

Stay Thirsty

God is never actually mentioned by name in the book of Esther. But throughout the story, we see Esther quietly responding to what I believe must surely have been God's whispers. Besides, I don't think the Lord would have entrusted the very survival of the children of Israel into the hands of a teenager unless He knew she would listen and obey.

I've come to believe that training our hearts to hear God's voice is one of our most important jobs as believers.[5] We do this primarily through reading God's Word and spending time in prayer. Esther must have learned to hear and obey God during her years under the watchful eye of Mordecai. Perhaps that is where she also grew to appreciate the power of fasting and prayer.

Somehow she managed to stay thirsty for God even while serving as queen. Her dramatic three-day fast put her in a place of utter dependency. And in the end, it brought great power to her petition for the deliverance of her people.

I have found fasting to be a useful weapon in my own prayer arsenal. Fasting seems to clear my thoughts and help me to focus my attention completely on God. Although I still have much to learn, I've noticed fasting sometimes seems to add strength and power to my prayers.

The combination of fasting and prayer has resulted in a couple of what I consider to be spiritual breakthroughs in long-standing problems. But fasting doesn't always have to be about not eating. In Isaiah 58 we read about a powerful type of fast when we pour our lives out to the spiritually and physically hungry of the world (verse 10). Or as one friend discovered, an increased sensitivity to God's voice when she went on a fast from social media. Fasting is simply one way of seeking God wholeheartedly, staying thirsty for Him.

Several years ago, David and I were invited to teach a group of men and women church leaders in Burundi about prayer. Burundi is a tiny nation in central Africa, referred to as Rwanda's twin. Its people suffered a lengthy civil war, much like the horrific genocide in Rwanda, only more hidden from the eyes of the world.

We shared biblical insights we had learned over the years and allowed time at the end for questions. A man raised his hand, stood up, and asked me, "Why did you not talk about fasting?" I looked around at their faces. I knew food was not always plentiful there. How could I talk about fasting when I wasn't sure they had enough to eat? But I underestimated the spiritual fervor of those men and women, all survivors of the genocide. They shared dramatic stories of how God had intervened in their lives in miraculous ways, stories of provision and deliverance from evil attacks during the war. And I began to learn what a powerful tool fasting can be for believers in broken places—or for any believer when we face our own broken places.

Jesus assumed believers would fast. He instructed them not to parade it before men when [not if] they fasted (Matthew 6:16-18). On another occasion, when explaining to His disciples why they couldn't cast out a demon from a young boy, He explained, "This kind can come out by nothing but prayer and fasting" (Mark 9:29 NKJV).

> The combination of fasting and prayer can help us strengthen our faith as women of valor.

The examples of Esther and our friends in Africa, along with the words of Jesus Himself, remind us that the combination of fasting and prayer can help us strengthen our faith as women of valor.

Only by Prayer and Fasting

You may be wondering if fasting still gets results today. I hope to encourage you with a story about one of the first times I fasted. The problem I faced could have become a serious one. In the end, there was a breakthrough, with a humorous twist that still makes me smile. Yet the episode opened my eyes to the power of prayer and fasting. It happened when my now 22-year-old son was nearly two.

After the birth of a beautiful daughter and a fine, strong son, David and I still felt as though our family wasn't finished. We had agonized through years of infertility before having our first two children, but we still hoped for a third. People wondered why we would put ourselves through the anguish and expense of more infertility treatments when we already had a daughter and a son. I could only describe it by saying it was as if someone was "trying to come to us." And sure enough, just a couple of months shy of my fortieth birthday, our little Michael made his entrance into this world.

Our lives, which had become fairly predictable with a nine-year-old and almost six-year-old, took a detour back to the world of diapers and midnight feedings. Things were made somewhat easier by the fact that Michael was a happy child. But he was also active, curious, and *always* into something. I had to call Poison Control three times after he swallowed a penny, drank a bottle of eardrops, and ate half a tube of toothpaste—all in one week. This is still a family record.

Michael began developing sinus infections that were resistant to repeated antibiotics the winter before his second birthday. After dealing with nearly six weeks of off-and-on sickness, this 40-something mother of a toddler grew weary and exhausted by the lack of sleep. Doctors were baffled. They recommended X-rays to determine the cause of the infections.

Out of desperation, I decided to fast for our son. I had little experience with fasting, but I was at the end of my rope. I wasn't even sure how one even did such a thing, but I resolved not to eat for 24 hours. When I felt hunger pangs throughout the day, I went to God over and over with the same simple prayer: "Help, Lord. I'm weary and frustrated. Surely You know what is causing these infections. Please show me!"

After naptime, I let Michael venture outside to play for a little while. It was unusually warm for February and he had been cooped up for days. A few minutes later, he ran inside, pointing to his nose. I thought he just wanted me to wipe it. But looking closer I caught my breath. A partially lodged brass pin-back, the kind used to fasten a sports insignia, was sticking out of Michael's left nostril! I gently removed the badly tarnished (and very gross) piece of metal. Suddenly, it dawned on me that *this* was the culprit of our 40-day ordeal! Our pediatrician later told me that brass is a "dirty" metal, and if the object (which, for weeks, had eluded all his examinations) had continued its migration to Michael's upper sinus cavity near the brain, our outcome could have been dangerous.

When I asked Michael how the thing got into his nose, he explained—in toddler language—how he'd climbed out of his crib one night and crawled up on his big brother's bed. Then he unfastened a sports pin from his brother's baseball cap and stuck the pin-back in his nose. Seriously?

We stood there in the kitchen, Michael and I, half-laughing and half-crying. I could hardly believe what had just happened. And right at that moment, a calm yet somewhat amused inner voice seemed to whisper the same words Jesus once spoke to His disciples. Words I have never forgotten: "This kind only comes out by prayer and fasting."

Stick Together

Esther was desperate for God to save her people. But in her humility, she knew better than to fight her battle alone. She gathered her army around her to fervently seek God for deliverance. Esther understood the power of *together*.

How about you? Do you "stick together" with other believers? Jesus reminds us that when two or three are gathered together for prayer *in*

His name, there's great power (Matthew 18:19-20). Again and again, He encourages followers to join together. He reminds believers everywhere: Don't fight this fight alone.

Psychologists have coined the term *isolation sickness* to tell us what we already know: It's harmful to our mental and emotional health when we become isolated from one another.[6] They point to certain patterns that warn us we need the company of others. Isolation sickness gives rise to behavior like paranoia or being overly sensitive to criticism, or to catastrophic thinking—making mountains out of molehills. Even followers of Christ can slip into living in too much isolation if we're not careful. Social media has compounded this risk. Plus, we're just plain more prone to sin when not accountable to other believers. We need each other to be strong.

> We need each other to stay strong and win our wars.

I encourage you to consider what you do to stay connected with other believers. Are you part of a small-group Bible study? Who is your army? (Maybe you could do the "Valor Quest" study at the back of this book with some friends.) The Bible reminds us to "encourage one another daily" so that we don't get "hardened by sin's deceitfulness" (Hebrews 3:13). Bottom line? As women of valor, we need each other if we want to stay strong and win our wars.

Stand Your Ground

Esther fasted. She gathered her army. She knew when to be silent and when to speak. She knew how to remain firm in her faith as she waited upon God. Or as I like to put it, she knew "when to say it and when to pray it." I feel sure she was listening intently for God's wisdom concerning how and when to approach the king to reveal the sinister plot against her people. She remained firm in her faith, trusting God and stepping out in obedience at just the right time. In short, Esther knew how to stand her ground.

Do you listen to God before you take action? I confess that I sometimes rush in and try to fix everything—just in case God "forgets" to handle it, and never with good results.

We've observed that by fasting, watching, and waiting for the right opportunity, Esther allowed God to move quietly behind the scenes and orchestrate a magnificent deliverance for the Jews. She grew stronger as she was intentional to stay thirsty for God, stick together with her community, and stay firm in her faith. Once again, we see that when one ordinary woman seeks and obeys God—and stands her ground as a woman of valor—extraordinary things can happen.

Our Real Source of Strength

How did such a young woman do battle with diabolical forces that attempted to wipe every Jew from the face of the earth—and win? How did she become so strong?

Esther's strength was rooted in her weakness. In her utter dependency upon God. "And if I perish, I perish" has gone on to become the battle cry for courageous warriors—both men and women—throughout history. Perhaps God chose Esther simply because He knew she would depend on Him completely.

Let's remind ourselves that though Esther's enemies took shape in the evil characters around her, the real battle was against the unseen forces in the spiritual realm—the same devil who has been trying to destroy God's people from day one. Esther's story is one of intense spiritual warfare.

That's why her real battle was to trust God. To believe He had called her into this exalted position "for such a time as this." To believe He could do the impossible and deliver the Jews. To believe He would give her a plan and the strength to carry out that plan. To believe He would keep her alive. Her real fight was the fight of faith.

As we continue our quest to be women of valor, let's remember the previous lesson from our Proverbs 31 woman. We're told the real

> Relationship with God is the foundation for life, the secret of strength, the reason for impact.

source of her strength near the end of the chapter: "Charm is deceptive, and beauty is fleeting; but a woman who fears the LORD is to be praised" (verse 30).

Like every true woman of valor, her relationship with God is the foundation for her life, the secret of strength, the reason for her impact. And like Esther, she is a fierce fighter for the faith. But if she, or any other woman of valor, is to fight effectively and finish her race well, she must learn to strengthen herself in the Lord.

If this is true, then—if we have a giant task at hand, a war to fight, a world to change—we need to reclaim our calling as women of valor. Let's dare to renew our grasp of this beautiful biblical concept that went missing in action.

And let's set about the task of making ourselves strong, whether through prayer, studying God's Word, gathering with other believers, or even fasting.

The Bible tells us the Lord is pleased when we search for Him wholeheartedly. "You will seek me and find me when you seek me with all your heart" (Jeremiah 29:13). If we get disconnected from God as our real source of strength, any of us can stumble and fall. Even as believers, we need to be on guard and stay strong in the Lord. We need to be extra strong because there is an enemy who hates us.

It's time to stop losing those wars we should be winning. We see this same truth played out again and again, so it's worth repeating: The most important fight for the woman of valor is the fight of faith. To prepare for battle, it's our job to strengthen ourselves in the Lord. Daily. Continually. Where that fight takes us and the work we're called to do is entirely up to God.

3

She Laughs at the Future

She is clothed with strength and dignity;
she can laugh at the days to come.

PROVERBS 31:25

looked at the dozen or so Iraqi women seated around me as they
engaged in lively conversation. Judging by all the joy and laughter in
the room, it was hard to believe they were recent refugees from Iraq.

It was our second mission trip to that area of the Middle East to
observe the work of Christian relief organizations. We'd visited several
of the countless refugee camps throughout Lebanon. I had met women
of both Muslim and Christian backgrounds, all fleeing the ravages of
ISIS and forced to make a home for their families in a strange land. In
their own way, these women—much like Esther—were exiles.

A friend who ministers to this particular group of Iraqi women said
I could expect to be surprised when I met them. Yes, they had fled for
their lives like other refugees in that area. Everyone was displaced and
surviving from day to day, burdened by the same intense stress of providing for their families. But these Iraqi women, she had discovered,
were unusual. Despite their extreme hardships, they always took pains

to dress nicely and create lovely homes—even if those homes were
in a crumbling apartment building or a crowded tent. And, she had
noticed, they always wore makeup.

I was intrigued to learn more. Before the morning was over, these
women would emerge in my eyes as shining examples of women of
valor.

David and I were grateful to be invited to their small-group Bible
study. Housing for refugees in the crowded city was hard to come by.
We met several of the women at a designated intersection and walked
together to the home of one of the women. She lived in a run-down
apartment building with peeling paint and cracked plaster walls.

But my friend was right. I could tell our hostess had worked especially hard to make her surroundings lovely. One wall was wallpapered
with a pattern of gold flowers on a burgundy background. A colorful rug was on the floor. Here and there, a few accessories—items she
must have quickly gathered before fleeing Iraq—adorned the walls
and shelves of the small living room. She served a flavorful tea and a
cake she'd baked especially for the group. The women were vibrant and
friendly, and despite the language barrier, we felt warmly welcomed. I
couldn't help but notice the special care they had given to their clothing and attractively styled hair. And yes, all wore makeup.

The women, I learned, had been nominal Catholics back in Iraq.
This was their very first Bible study. They were enthusiastic students,
and it was clear that the Word of God had become an anchor for them
during their traumatic uprooting. They seemed to enjoy the small-
group atmosphere, and it was obvious they had grown to love and
support each other. First, they shared prayer requests and prayed for
one another—mostly about family concerns. I could sense how much
strength they drew from prayer.

Then they launched into their study of the book of Genesis. That
morning they were talking about the story of Jacob and how he found

a wife (Genesis 29:14-30). I'd heard the story many times, but never quite like this.

If you're familiar with the story, you'll remember that Jacob falls in love with beautiful Rachel, the younger daughter of his distant relative, Laban. He arranges to work for seven years in return for Rachel's hand in marriage. The big day arrives, but on the wedding night, Laban tricks Jacob and gives him Leah as his bride instead.

As you might imagine, Jacob is shocked the next morning to discover that he has married not his beautiful Rachel, but Leah, the less attractive older sister. Laban insists that Jacob work seven more years to marry his beloved Rachel. At this point, the women launched into an animated conversation and shared insights about Jacob and his complex family. It seemed impossible to them that such a thing could have happened to poor Jacob.

Now, I'd always felt sorry for Jacob, too, especially since I thought he had to wait another seven years before he got to marry Rachel—14 years of work in all. "Oh no!" the women exclaimed. "Jacob was able to marry Rachel at the end of that week. He only had to wait seven days. Then he worked for seven more years *after* he married Rachel." And there erupted the lovely, musical female chatter common to women everywhere when engaged in a lively debate. My husband, ever the Bible scholar, said he had also thought Jacob had to wait seven more years before he got Rachel.

"No, look right here," insisted their group leader, pointing firmly to her Arabic Bible. Translating for us, our interpreter explained that the women were absolutely certain Jacob finished his wedding week with Leah and then married his true love, Rachel. Yes, he did have to work seven more years, but he married Rachel *first*.

Sure enough, as we looked closer at our English Bibles, we realized they were absolutely right. Laban only required Jacob to finish Leah's bridal week before he could have Rachel as his bride "in return for another seven years of work" (Genesis 29:27). Verse 28 says, "[Jacob] finished the week with Leah, and then Laban gave him his daughter Rachel to be his wife." David and I laughed. It meant so much to these women to know that God did not make poor Jacob wait 14 years for his beloved—they wanted a happy ending.

My purpose in telling you about my morning with the Iraqi women is not simply to give insights into the story of Jacob and his unusual weddings. Rather, I want you to imagine the atmosphere with our new Iraqi friends, rich with laughter and camaraderie. Perhaps you'll be better able to grasp the strength and courage of these women—and why I found their joy so astounding—when I tell you what happened next.

Stunned by Their Stories

We had enjoyed our visit for over an hour and our time was wrapping up when one of the Iraqi women said, "Would you like to hear some of our personal stories?"

"Of course," we all replied. The woman next to me began to share her story. "My husband was kidnapped by ISIS and tortured for ten days," she said, somewhat matter-of-factly. Then she pulled out her cell phone as though she were going to show me pictures of her family. "Look," she said, pointing and scrolling through the photos. "Here's where they put cigarette burns on his feet."

"They took my son, too," she added, "but both are back safely with me now." She seemed calm. She was eager to talk, but there wasn't a trace of fear in her voice.

Another chimed in, "Yes, back in Iraq, we had a nice house and three cars. One day our Muslim neighbors came to our home and told us we had to leave or they would kill us." Her family quickly fled with only what they could pack in one car. Now they were trying hard to adapt to life as refugees in a strange new city.

I was still trying to process all this when the attractive blonde woman across from me said quietly, "Members of ISIS killed my husband and my son in a car bomb." She paused, and added, "My son was only 23." I thought of our own two sons back home, also in their twenties, but far away from war.

I listened intently as these women told their stories. But inwardly I was reeling, caught off guard given the lightheartedness of our earlier conversations. I was also struck by the lack of self-pity with which they described their trauma. I sensed their suffering was not without meaning for them. As one woman put it, "Our hardships have opened the door for us to know Jesus and to study the Bible for the very first time. And we have been blessed to be in this group together." Others joined in, talking about how they had drawn strength from the Lord and from each other.

Their outward circumstances were out of their control, even tragic. But these women had managed to create a fragment of order—and yes, beauty—for their families. They had become a community of survivors. They were nurturers and warriors, these women of valor.

I know of no quick answers or steps of action to help us replicate what the Lord miraculously provided to help these women endure their sufferings. I personally believe His gift of grace is the kind of extraordinary grace you get only when you need it—when you are truly in the fiery furnace. But we can draw strength

> There was something almost holy about their laughter in the middle of their terrible trials.

from their example of courage, their resolve, and their love. And once again, I am reminded of this: The woman of valor often shines brightest in times of war.

Laughter as a Weapon

Let's take another look at our Proverbs 31 woman. We're told "she is clothed with strength and dignity; she can laugh at the days to come" (verse 25). This verse comes alive for me whenever I remember the sounds of the Iraqi women's laughter—a sound that reverberated with faith, not fear. Trust, not terror. It's true that they were clothed with "strength and dignity." But it was their laughter that surprised me. I agree with the woman who once said her favorite emotion was "laughter through tears." There was something almost holy about their laughter in the middle of their terrible trials.

When you pause to consider what these Iraqi women have endured, they should not be laughing. Sighing or crying, maybe. But laughing? It was as if their laughter was a show of force. These women were intentional—they were not letting their circumstances defeat them. Or define them. They refused to give in to fear and allow the Enemy to win. In that respect, their laughter was a war cry. It's been said that joy is the flag that flies over the castle when the king is on his throne. If that's the case, then maybe laughter is the victory dance.

The word translated *laugh* in Proverbs 31:25 has this celebratory flavor: "to laugh, be amused, celebrate, rejoice."[1] It can even mean to mock or scoff, as when one laughs at his vanquished enemies.

This sort of laughter has a touch of a swagger that says, "We have won!" It's the same word used to describe Sarah's laugh when she learned she would have a son; and then after he was born, she laughed again (Genesis 18). In fact, the name *Isaac* means "laughter." Just imagine the victory sounds rippling through Abraham's tent at the birth of the son through whom the nations of the world would be blessed.

History is filled with accounts of courageous men and women who managed to smile or even laugh in the most desperate of circumstances. This was true in the concentration camps of World War II. When one Jewish prisoner was asked by the Nazis if he would like a cigarette before he was shot by the firing squad, he is said to have quipped, "No thanks; it's bad for my health." Humor was one way the prisoners were able to say to their captors, "We are not defeated."

Laughter is combat. Refusal to surrender to the Enemy. It's the banner raised out of the dust heap of death, which cries out, "You have not won. My God reigns."

One of the reasons I'm writing this book is to introduce you to everyday women of valor who are quietly, bravely fighting battles. They're caring for their families and for their communi-

> Laughter is combat.

ties. Some, like the Iraqi refugees, are carving out a new life in a strange land. They are the unsung heroes of war. And they can be found all over the world wherever there are hard times and hard places. They can encourage us in our own times of trial to be brave. To stand firm. To be women of valor right where we are.

We may not be war refugees, but we all suffer grief and loss as we go through life. We all must fight the fight of faith, sometimes through our tears. Just as we did Esther, let's continue to draw strength from their stories. Perhaps we can learn how to stand firm in our faith—and maybe even laugh a little—during our own tough times.

A Dangerous Enemy

I left my encounter with my new Iraqi friends inspired, but also wondering why I sometimes don't stand stronger when going through my own trials. After seeing firsthand the mighty ways God is at work in extreme circumstances, I want to enlarge my view of Him. And like any good warrior, I need to become familiar with the tactics of the Enemy.

Women in my corner of the world seem to struggle with worry and anxiety more than women in dangerous places. I even had a couple of friends back home tell me they were getting counseling because they were so afraid of ISIS. They appeared to be more terrified of terror attacks than the women who have actually survived them.

Please don't misunderstand. I don't want to make light of anxiety. It's a real problem. I don't have to tell you that among people everywhere, anxiety is on the rise. Maybe you've struggled with worries and fears at times. I know I have.

But let's face it. Women of every generation have had to deal with fear. Just raising a family brings the temptation to worry. It seems to come with the territory when we love people. Some of us are more prone to worry than others, an unfortunate aspect of our genetic makeup. Plus, social media puts us face-to-face with far more concerns than we were ever meant to carry. Anxiety is a subtle but dangerous enemy.

Some anxiety is normal, even useful. The added alertness produces adrenaline, which provides us with the heightened readiness to solve problems or take action against danger. But extreme anxiety takes a toll on our brains and our bodies. Chemical changes keep the feel-good neurotransmitters in our brains from doing their work, so they can cause sleeping and digestive problems, headaches, increased blood pressure, or even mimic a heart attack.

My background is in counseling, and I've worked with women in the local church for nearly 40 years. I'm especially concerned at the toll anxiety is taking on women of all ages and stages. In talking with a friend who counsels those with anxiety, she commented on the many practical and positive ways she encourages her clients to lessen its impact—like getting regular exercise, eating healthy food, getting adequate rest, spending time with friends, taking up a hobby, or even taking a nap. (I'll share what I've discovered to be the "perfect nap" in chapter 7.)

Sadly, some sufferers drift to destructive ways to detach from anxiety, such as addictions, unhealthy relationships, overeating, or even overwork. Perhaps that's why research professor and author, Brené Brown, has called us "the most in debt, obese, addicted, medicated adult cohort in American history."[2]

I'm convinced that fear is at the root of so many of our issues, and it's no wonder Jesus reminds us again and again to "fear not." He tells us, "Do not worry about your life, what you will eat or drink; or about your body, what you will wear" (Matthew 6:25) but rather to "seek first his kingdom and his righteousness, and all these things will be given to you as well. Therefore do not worry about tomorrow" (verses 33-34). Jesus knew full well that anxiety is the enemy of faith.

Don't Worry; Instead, Pray

We've talked about laughter as a weapon against anxiety. Another personal favorite when it comes to dealing with fear and worry is prayer. I am a born worrier, and I've struggled with this problem much of my life.

Several years ago, I read a couple of Bible verses that changed the way I deal with worry by transforming the way I pray. God's Word can do that, you know.

The first verse hit hard right in the middle of my furrowed brow: "Don't worry about anything; instead, pray about everything. Tell God what you need, and thank him for all he has done" (Philippians 4:6 NLT). Verse 7 packed an equally powerful punch, promising that after we pray in this way, "then you will experience God's peace, which exceeds anything we can understand. His peace will guard your hearts and minds as you live in Christ Jesus."

Wow. I was challenged to take all that wound-up energy I was spending on worry, and "instead" hurl it back to the Lord in prayer. It reminded me of the time I visited Niagara Falls and observed the spectacular energy of the rushing water harnessed to provide electrical power for millions of homes in the United States and Canada.

Or even better—since we are talking about being warriors—is the example of when I took karate back in high school. We were instructed to redirect our attacker's own power into a counterattack—right back at the very enemy who was coming after us. In a similar way, turning our worry into prayer is like a one-two punch into the solar plexus of our enemy, Satan.

In light of what I learned from these verses,

> Turning our worry into prayer is like a one-two punch into the solar plexus of our enemy, Satan.

I began to develop a simple but powerful way to pray. I'll spell it out for you in more detail in chapter 5.[3] But for now, why not begin to turn your worry into energy for prayer? Or as the famous nineteenth-century British pastor Charles Spurgeon said, "Turn your cares into prayers."[4]

Friend, it's time to be ruthless warriors. We simply must win the war on worry if we hope to rise up as women of valor. What if we treated anxiety, and its cohorts of fear and worry, as the diabolical threats they are? I've come to see fear as perhaps the singular most insidious intruder crippling the woman of valor—taking the fight out of her and rendering her defenseless. It's time to stand up and fight back. God has given us everything we need to win this war.

Let's take a look at another powerful weapon we can use to fight anxiety. Like the Proverbs 31 woman of valor, let's learn to "laugh at the days to come."

Joy: The Antidote to Anxiety

Laughter and joy are closely related. And while laughter is an outward expression, I like to think of joy as the inner attitude of the mind. My friend Heather first got me thinking about the power of joy to disarm anxiety. I had always considered the opposite of anxiety to be *peace*. Thus my previous way of dealing with anxiety had been to struggle for peace and stop there. Joy, I was to learn, can help us win a much more decisive victory over anxiety.

Heather had experienced lots of anxiety in her early twenties. As she put it, "My life was coming at me from all angles, and I realized I had no one to turn to but my God!"

Heather began to write down Bible verses to give her comfort, and she realized that most of them revolved around joy. "I began to understand that *joy*, and not simply peace, was the opposite of anxiety," she

said. "I felt like anxiety was the result of trying to carry my own burdens. And it was robbing me of the joy God so desperately wanted
to give me."

> "*Joy*, and not
> simply peace,
> is the opposite
> of anxiety."

Heather discovered more than 70 references
to joy in the New Testament alone. She would post the verses on sticky
notes in various places as a reminder to cast her burdens on the Lord and
receive His joy in their place. She sent me a few verses that she began to
meditate on and still clings to many years later. She began to find victory
over her anxiety as she was reminded to "rejoice in our sufferings, knowing that suffering produces endurance" (Romans 5:3 ESV). Or to be "joyful in hope, patient in affliction, faithful in prayer" (Romans 12:12).

The Bible teaches us there is great power in this kind of joy. "The joy
of the LORD is your strength," Nehemiah reminded the exiles who were
returning from their years of captivity in Babylon (Nehemiah 8:10).

As we explore how joy can be a weapon, let's take a deeper look at
the word *anxiety* in the New Testament. The Greek word *merimna* can
be translated as *worry* or *anxiety*. That word comes from two words,
which mean "divided" and "mind." It helps to think of anxiety as a
"divided mind" or a "broken mind." Perhaps that sheds some light on
old expressions for extreme mental anxiety: "nervous breakdown" and
"cracking up."

Here's where joy comes in and why it can be a good way to fight
fear and anxiety. In Scripture, a couple of different words can be translated as *joy*. We see one of those here: "You have made known to me
the paths of life; you will fill me with joy in your presence" (Acts 2:28).

The Greek word translated as *joy* in this verse is *euphrosyne*. It comes
from two words: The prefix *eu* means "good, or well." The word *phren*
means "mind." I love to think of joy as more than a feeling—it's a *well
mind*. A healthy mind, as opposed to a broken mind. In that respect,
then, joy is the opposite of anxiety. Now you see why joy can be an
antidote to anxiety.

Some women who happened to be Greek Orthodox once heard me mention this Greek word for joy. They came up immediately after the message and said, "Yes, you are right about the word *euphrosyne*. What's more," they told me, "a common Greek name for women is *Euphie*, which comes from this same word." I like to think of the name *Euphie* when I see the word *joy*.

Doctors have discovered that joy—and the laughter that goes with it—has a healing effect on our minds and our bodies. There's even something called "laughter therapy," which claims success because it lowers blood pressure and heart rate and increases endorphins. It would appear that joy is good for us mentally, physically, and spiritually.

> Joy is a well mind.

To review, we see that laughter is linked to joy. It is an outward expression of the joy that lives in the mind. And joy makes women strong. It makes our minds healthy. Joy also strengthens us for the battles we face every day as women of valor.

Praise Gives Power

Joy directed into praise could be called *worship*. As we saw earlier, the Proverbs 31 woman "rejoices over the future" (verse 25 AMPC). Rejoicing over the future sounds a lot like praise to me.

No one can measure the spiritual power found in praising God. Praise is like waving the victory banner over the head of the Enemy. The Bible tells us the Lord dwells in the praises of His people (Psalm 22:3). A friend of mine from Africa puts it this way: "Singing praise to God is like praying *twice*." Singing praises to God is also a weapon, she added, driving fear and worry from our minds.

Yet for all its power, praise is something so simple even a child can practice it. "From the lips of children and infants you, Lord, have called forth your praise" (Matthew 21:16). Little Willie Myrick is one of my heroes. I like to think of him as a young man of valor. Willie discovered firsthand the enormous power of praise to defeat the Enemy.

When he was ten years old, Willie was kidnapped from his home in Atlanta by a knife-wielding assailant. His kidnapper placed a ten-dollar bill as "bait" at the foot of a tree near Willie's driveway. When the curious youngster reached down to pick it up, the man sprang from behind the tree, grabbed Willie, and forced him into a car. Speeding across town with the little boy in the backseat, the man spewed profanity and threats.

The frightened ten-year-old decided to sing his favorite worship song, "Every Praise."[5] When Willie was later asked why he sang this particular song, he told news reporters, "Well, because I knew Jesus was gonna be with me and he was gonna get me out!"

Willie continued to sing the song—for three hours! The man finally stopped the car, still cursing and shouting threats, and shoved Willie out unharmed. Just imagine the warrior-like faith of this young boy. Instead of dissolving into tears or panic, he praised and worshiped God!

I was so inspired by Willie's story that now, when faced with worry or fear, I'm trying to remember to respond with praise. Just the other day a troubling situation arose that tempted me to fall into worry. An old hymn—one I hadn't thought of in years—suddenly came to mind. The words to "A Mighty Fortress Is Our God" poured forth like a warrior's march. I literally turned my back on my problem and used the song to focus on God's power. Sure enough, my mental climate changed when I began to give thanks and praise—the back of fear was broken. What's more, the situation that had worried me so much resolved itself.

Whenever my worry doesn't lift right away, or a problem persists, I have to remind myself that Willie Myrick kept singing his simple praise song for three hours before he was released! "Rejoice always," the Bible reminds us. "Pray continually, give thanks in all circumstances; for this is God's will for you in Christ Jesus" (1 Thessalonians 5:16-18).

As women of valor, let's take a lesson from a brave ten-year-old and become women of praise. God's Word promises that praise helps us stand our ground in the face of the Enemy.

A Mighty Fortress Is Our God

A mighty fortress is our God, a bulwark never failing;
Our helper he amid the flood of mortal ills prevailing.
For still our ancient foe doth seek to work us woe;
His craft and power are great and armed with cruel hate,
On earth is not his equal.

Did we in our own strength confide, our striving would be
    losing,
Were not the right man on our side, the man of God's own
    choosing.
Dost ask who that may be? Christ Jesus, it is he;
Lord Sabaoth, his name, from age to age the same,
And he must win the battle.

And though this world, with devils filled, should threaten to
    undo us,
We will not fear, for God hath willed his truth to triumph
    through us.
The Prince of Darkness grim, we tremble not for him;
His rage we can endure, for lo, his doom is sure;
One little word shall fell him.

That word above all earthly powers, no thanks to them,
    abideth;
The Spirit and the gifts are ours, thro' him who with us sideth.
Let goods and kindred go, this mortal life also;
The body they may kill; God's truth abideth still;
His kingdom is forever.[6]

Trials Bring More Joy

"What doesn't kill you makes you stronger." I always figured this quote was true, but I secretly hoped I'd never have to find out. Of course, in time, we all discover life can hit hard. Some problems don't seem to budge, no matter how hard we pray. We wonder if we can endure.

But it's also true that surviving trials—walking through hard places—is another way we grow stronger. And some of life's most difficult experiences can be the tools God uses to shape us into women of valor. What's more, as we learned from the Iraqi refugees, sometimes joy, and even laughter, can spring up in the midst of our fiery trials.

I know my own faith was strengthened and refined during a long struggle with infertility. I don't have the space here to share all the details about what ended up being nine years of praying, medical treatments, surgeries, and even a miracle of healing before the births of our three children. But I will tell you that many years later I still draw from the lessons I learned—and the joy I discovered—during those difficult years of waiting.

Perhaps you can point to your own stories of how you grew stronger through fighting your own fight of faith. Or maybe you're in the middle of a fiery trial right now. But God loves to strengthen us during the storm—promising to give us an unexplainable joy as we trust in Him. That's why the Bible encourages us to "consider it pure joy" when we encounter trials, since that's when our faith is tested and even strengthened (James 1:2). These same trials help us learn to persevere, which in turn builds our character. This gives rise to hope, and hope does not leave us disappointed (Romans 5:3-5).

Over the years, I have noticed that strength often comes when we, as women, lose control over the externals of life and have to dig deep to draw our strength from God. It's true that we tend to lean into God more during our times of suffering. In such times, even the words of Scripture seem to jump off the page and find their way into our hearts. A friend of mine who walked through losing several family members in an accident told me it was only God's Word that sustained her. "I grew to love God's Word so much I would eat the pages of the Bible if I could," she said, smiling. Sounds like Jeremiah, who cried out to the Lord in his suffering, "When your words came, I ate them; they were my joy and my heart's delight" (Jeremiah 15:16).

During times of trial, we are compelled to enlarge our view of God. To see Him at work brings confidence and dispels worry. It strengthens our faith. Perhaps that's why I have found some of God's strongest men and women of valor, like the Iraqi women, in places where life is more dangerous and enemies are ever present.

> God's supernatural brand of joy lives and breathes through our minds.

We can draw strength from their testimonies, knowing that the same God loves us, too, and is ready to help us in our hard places. He wants us to trust Him, for He is always ready to strengthen us in our moments of feeling lost and alone, discouraged or without hope.

Let's remember that God's supernatural brand of joy lives and breathes through our minds. It casts out fear. It helps us to face our future with faith. That's why we, too, can laugh at the days to come.

No Fear Except the Fear of the Lord

Joy—expressed through laughter and praise—is a powerful weapon in the hands of a woman. We've seen that joy is an attitude of the mind, while laughter is an outward demonstration of that joy. *Praise* directs joy toward God in worship. More importantly, these same weapons strengthen our faith and drive out fear.

It's clear that joy was present in the life of the Proverbs 31 woman of valor. She must have learned to overcome anxiety so she could "laugh at the days to come." Or as another Bible version puts it, "She looks to the future with confidence."

Some scholars believe the woman in Proverbs 31 was able to face her future with confidence because of her hard work in establishing an orderly and well-prepared home. She had gathered ample stores, and consequently was ready for any kind of problem she or her family might face—whether that was harsh weather, famine, villains, or disease.

This may be true. But I like to think that over the years she had also learned to laugh at the future because of her deep faith in God—a woman we're told who "fears the LORD" (verse 30). Remember, it's likely she is a mature woman by the time we read about her. She had no doubt seen God work through many of her problems. She knew she could trust Him to provide whatever she needed in the days ahead. That's why she could face her future with an attitude of joy. I especially like the way The Living Bible paraphrases verse 25: "She is a woman of strength and dignity and has no fear of old age."

But let's not forget that at its core, *valor* is a military term. If we want to face our future with confidence, free from fear, we must be ready for spiritual battles. Because as I keep repeating, whether or not we like it, we are at war. We live on enemy soil.

God has placed us on earth to do His work. It's a privilege and a calling, but a battle nonetheless. Yet a battle the Bible calls the "good fight." In his book *Champagne for the Soul*, Mike Mason challenges us with these words:

> The secret of winning at spiritual warfare is to love it. One must love war the way soccer players love soccer, with a savage alacrity. One must love the battle itself, the surge of adrenaline, the feeling of strength and skill. If we want joy, we'll have to fight for it, deliberately and fiercely...Waging war in Christ's name is not an oppressive duty but a royal privilege integrally linked to joy. Our Warrior God wants us to know the pleasure not only of winning, but of fighting itself. If we shrink from struggles we abdicate part of our humanity. To be fully alive is to plow full-steam into life,

acknowledging all of it, horrors included. No joy comes to
us through denying evil but only through...fighting under
Christ's banner against sin, the world, and the devil.[7]

We grow strong as women of valor, knowing that the way we fight
our fight of faith will make an impact on the lives of those around us.
Therefore, we should continually remind ourselves that if we want to
be clothed with "strength and dignity" and "laugh at the future," we
must daily, hourly, work to make ourselves strong—strong in the Lord.

My favorite verse on spiritual warfare is short and simple: "Submit
to God. Resist the devil and he will flee from you" (James 4:7 NKJV).
To submit to God is fighting the right fight—the fight of the faith
(1 Timothy 6:12). We submit by staying thirsty for God and obedient
to His Word, by praying and fasting, and by sticking together with our
fellow believers, as we learned from Esther in the previous chapter. We
resist the devil by standing our ground, filling our minds with joy, and
expressing this joy through praise, or maybe even laughter.

All of this strengthens us as women of valor who endure our hardships with hope. Let's dare to become an army of women who, in the
words of John Wesley, "hate nothing but sin and fear nothing but God."
This is how we do war.

The Bible reminds us to build our personal faith, our "spiritual
house," on the solid rock of our relationship with Jesus Christ (Matthew 7:24-27). We must remain vigilant to keep that house "swept
clean" of enemies like fear and anxiety. And if the fear of the Lord is
truly the "beginning of wisdom," as Psalm 111:10 reminds us, then let's
begin to explore some ways we can build our houses wisely.

4

She Builds Her House Wisely

The wise woman builds her house, but with her
own hands the foolish one tears hers down.

PROVERBS 14:1

Kerri Walsh Jennings sparked a firestorm of controversy at the 2016 Summer Olympics in Rio when she talked to a reporter about the importance of her family. "I feel like I was born to have babies and play volleyball," she said. The three-time Olympic gold medalist and mother of three went on to say she would love to win a fourth gold medal and have a fourth child. "My priorities are my faith, my family, and volleyball."[1]

Motherhood has helped Jennings put things in perspective, she explained, by moving her beyond a merely "self-centered" focus. Her husband and children have brought a certain balance to life that inspired her to take her game to the next level. While some applauded the athlete's courage, the Twitter world exploded with complaints that women should not have to be mothers to feel fulfilled.

I was intrigued by all the backlash, because here's the thing: Jennings did not say she couldn't play volleyball and be a mother. In fact, she was five weeks pregnant with her third child when she won her third Olympic gold in London back in 2012. Nor did she say women had to be mothers to be fulfilled. She simply said she felt she was made to be a mother and play volleyball. The scathing nature of the attacks centered on Jennings's comment that she was "born" to be a mother at all. Perhaps her critics would have been fine with Jennings as the strong volleyball player but not as the nurturing mother.

It seems that strength—more than maternal love—is beginning to mesmerize our increasingly self-absorbed culture. "Strength is seductive," touts the headline of a recent woman's magazine. Or "Strong is the new beautiful," promises a newly released book.[2] To which I would respond with this question: Strong for what purpose or for whom?

As we reflect on what it means to be a woman of valor, let's remember that God wants to make us strong so we can fight the battles He calls us to fight—primarily the fight of faith. But we are created to be both nurturers and warriors. God promises we'll find life as we give our lives away. Strong? Yes, but for the sake of others. And for a purpose that goes beyond ourselves.

My Change of Mind

I must pause here because I'm amused at finding myself in the role of champion for motherhood. But it's true; raising strong kids—who go on to become world-changers themselves—has been my master passion. Yet ironically, the first disagreement David and I had as a newly married couple was, of all things, about children. How many should we have? If we had children at all, I insisted, we should have no more than two.

Now, you'd think we would have approached this subject when dating. But we were married less than a year after our first date—a blind date at that. Needless to say, we still had some ground to cover concerning what our family should look like. I'd also gone from being an agnostic with feminist leanings to a believer in Jesus just a year before we met. I was very new in my faith and still wrestling through some of my ideas and beliefs. Perhaps you'll get a clearer picture if I rewind the clock to the week before that first date.

I was getting ready to move into my new apartment in Atlanta on that sweltering July morning so many years ago. Rhonda, my roommate, was expecting me before lunchtime. I had packed my car to the brim with clothes and boxes. But on my way across town, my car's water pump suddenly burst. After a three-hour repair, I finally pulled up to our apartment just as Rhonda's friend, Steve, was coming down the steps to leave.

I had never met Steve, but we exchanged quick hellos. He helped me unload an armload of clothes and a couple of boxes. Our interchange lasted maybe ten minutes. Parenthetically, if my water pump had not broken, we would never have crossed paths that day. Anyway, I never saw Steve again. But those ten minutes would change the course of my entire life.

I had just returned from an exciting summer internship with one of our Georgia senator's staff in Washington, DC. It was 1977, and I was awash in the memories of working on Capitol Hill. A little-known peanut farmer named Jimmy Carter, Georgia's former governor, had amazingly made his way to the White House. President Carter also happened to be the uncle of my college sorority's president. Another friend's sister had married President Carter's oldest son, so it all felt very close to home.

I had been assigned to the senator's press corps. And with my Georgia connections, I got an up-close-and-personal look at Washington politics—once visiting the family quarters of the White House. Heady stuff for a 21-year-old fresh out of college. World-changing decisions were made in that city. And since I, too, wanted to change the world, I was fascinated by it all. The internship fueled my passion to do something important with my life.

So there I was that summer day, moving into my Atlanta apartment, ready to start my position in public relations with a major company the following week. I unloaded the final boxes and thanked Steve for helping me out. And I breathed in the excitement of life in the big city, finally on my own.

What I didn't know is that right after our brief encounter, Steve approached one of his basketball buddies at their next practice and said something like this: "Hey, man, I met this girl when she was moving into her apartment. And I'm pretty sure you two are meant for each other. Seriously, man, your *auras* match." Steve smiled and handed his teammate a piece of paper on which he had hastily scribbled my first name and a phone number.

That "basketball buddy" happened to be David Chadwick, my husband of now nearly four decades. Good thing Steve was persistent in his attempts to set us up, because as David tells his side of the story, "The whole idea didn't excite me much at first. That aura stuff sounded a little 'New Age-y.'" (Remember, this was the seventies.) But Steve would not be thwarted. "To get him off my back," David says, laughing, "I finally decided to call this girl. We made a date to go rafting down the Chattahoochee River. All I can tell you is when I arrived to pick her up and she opened the door...suddenly I knew. She was the one."

And I quickly fell for the handsome, kindhearted, basketball-player-turned-preacher. Four months later, David and I were engaged. Nine months after our first date, we were married and on our way to Texas, where David would complete his doctorate in ministry internship at a large church in Houston. And the girl who swore she would never become a Christian and never, *ever* marry a minister was suddenly a preacher's wife.

Perhaps you can see now why my head was spinning. I was delighted to be married to David, but I wasn't sure if I was the maternal type. Plus, my company had graciously offered me a year's leave of absence and promised my position would still be there when we returned. So in my mind, children could wait.

A lot happened in that first year of marriage. I began studying the Bible in earnest and started a small group of young wives who were as new in their faith as I was. We were eager to grow strong in our marriages and open to whatever God wanted to teach us. As I grew closer to the Lord, my ideas about what was truly important in life began to gradually shift. I thrived on ministry with David and loved helping others. And I began to look forward to one day being a mother. I didn't know it then, but we would face a long and grueling battle with infertility before we finally had our three children.

Our years of waiting were not wasted. I partnered with David in those early years of building our church. I earned a master's degree in counseling, went on my first mission trip to Africa, and found joy working among the poor in our community.

But I desperately longed to be a mother. Year after year went by, and I eventually began to feel as though having a baby would be nothing short of a miracle. As it turned out, I experienced a rather dramatic physical healing—a story I'll share later. Let's just say that by the time that first baby arrived, after nearly eight years of marriage, I had become passionate about being a mother. I went from thinking, "You mean I've *got* to have a baby?" to crying out joyfully after learning I was pregnant, "You mean I *get* to have a baby?"

Who Is Your Household?

Now, I'm aware some of you reading this book are not mothers. Perhaps you're walking through your own difficult time of infertility. Or maybe you're not married. I don't want you to feel left out, for God's Word clearly teaches that regardless of your age and stage of life, whether you're married or single, you can have a powerful influence on those around you. Being a woman of valor is something you are— not something you do.

Deborah, a prophet who rose to lead Israel to victory, was referred to as "a mother in Israel." The Bible doesn't tell us whether she had children. Only that she had tremendous impact as a leader among her people, who daily sought her out for wisdom and leadership.[3]

We're talking in this chapter about how to build your house wisely. In Bible language, your house can mean your home and your family, or even your "spiritual house." But it can also mean your "household," the people you hold dear, whoever they may be.

One young blogger, who happens to be unmarried and Jewish, confessed she often felt left out when the *Eshet Chayil*, or "Woman of Valor" poem was read in her home each Friday night before Shabbat. That is, until she started looking at the woman of valor in a new way. "I had focused so much on how things appeared to other people that I neglected to give enough time to cultivate a trust in myself in service to the Creator."

She decided to change careers and took a job working with the homeless. She woke up every morning at 4:00 a.m. to work on the streets of Upper Manhattan, where she served the homeless, bringing mental health and drug addiction services along with generous doses of kindness and compassion.

She writes, "Cherishing the calm that washed over me in the quietness of New York City in the early morning, I read over the familiar words of *Eshet Chayil*, and to my surprise, the words resonated... The streets of New York had become my household and in their quiet whisper I was finally able to hear the voice I was searching for, along with the identity that comes from within. We are already Women of Valor," she realized. "Just the households we serve all look a bit different."[4]

> Single, married, widow, or teen, God is calling you to give your life to a broken world.

Whether you're married or single, a widow, an empty-nester, or even a teenager like Esther, God is calling you to give your life to a broken world. I don't know what your household looks like. But I encourage you to ask God to show you some practical ways to become a woman of valor—the warrior and nurturer—for those around you.

Family Really Matters

Stop for a minute and think about your house. How does it make you feel? Most women love their houses. They can tell you the story of how and why they selected their particular house. And if a woman participated in the actual design of the house, like I did, the building process became an all-consuming labor of love. Truly, home is where the heart is.

Or is it? Sadly, more than half of all homes today end up as broken homes. What's more, two-thirds of those divorces are now initiated by women. It would appear that it's easier to spend time, energy, and money on the outward appearance of our houses than on nurturing the families that live inside. More than ever, we need to learn how to build our homes wisely.

In the Bible, the words for "house" and "home" are interchangeable with the words for "family" or "generation." When a woman builds her home, she is building her family, her lineage, and her destiny.

Home—and the family—was God's idea from the very beginning. He created a man and a woman to be in a lifelong marriage raising children together. And this nuclear family—not the church or the government—was His intended building block for all of human society. Home was where individuals could be nurtured and faith ignited. Even the church was modeled after the family.

> "Marriage remains America's strongest anti-poverty weapon."

It's just plain common sense that the family is vital to a healthy community. Sociologists have long recognized that marriage is a safeguard against poverty. Having a strong marriage is a bigger predictor of whether someone will be poor than race, education, or socioeconomic group. "Child poverty is an ongoing national concern, but few are aware that its principal cause is the absence of married fathers in the home. Marriage remains America's strongest anti-poverty weapon."[5] What's more, of single parent, female-headed homes, 37 percent in America live in poverty. Of those that are married, just 6.8 percent.[6] That means a child living in a broken home is five times more likely to be poor. Not only is marriage a powerful weapon in fighting poverty, but being married has the same effect in reducing poverty as adding five to six years to a parent's level of education.[7]

Our families are worth fighting for. But as women of valor, we're not just fighters—we're also builders. We're much like Nehemiah, who rebuilt the wall after God's people returned home after years in the Babylonian exile. Nehemiah warned his builders to remain alert and ready for outside attack. They "did their work with one hand and held a weapon in the other" (Nehemiah 4:17).

We're to build our homes while watching out for enemies who would seek to destroy our families. To create strong homes in today's world requires a fight. And it requires building wisely. It's important to carefully consider how we build.

Build on Solid Rock

The Bible warns that our choices and actions, and even how we build, will have a tremendous impact—for good or evil—on those around us. "The wise woman builds her house, but with her own hands the foolish one tears hers down" (Proverbs 14:1). The word *house* in this verse can describe a tent, a hut, a mansion, or a palace. It can also mean a family, a household, or descendants.

> Our relationship with Christ is the foundation for building strong families and households.

It's true that God has provided everything we need to build strong households. But Scripture reminds us we must first build our own "spiritual house." We're encouraged to build on the solid rock of our relationship with Jesus Christ (Matthew 7:24-27).

I'll say it again: Our relationship with Christ is the foundation for building strong families and households. Let's remember that the "fear of the LORD" was at the core of the Proverbs 31 woman's fruitful life (verse 30). Ultimately, the best way to build your house is to first build your faith.

The Greek New Testament word translated as *build* is *oikodomeo*. In addition to the construction of an actual dwelling, *oikodomeo* can also mean "to build up, edify, strengthen, or develop another person's life through acts and words of love and encouragement."[8] It carries with it the idea of advancing a person's spiritual condition.

We're instructed to "encourage one another and build each other up" (1 Thessalonians 5:11). As a wife, a mother, and a friend, I am called to be a builder, not just of my own household, but also of others in the body of Christ.

So how do we build our own spiritual house? I believe there are some basic principles for how to do this, along with lots of flexibility to be creative. Clearly, one size does not fit all. I've experimented over the years, and for me, the morning quiet time of prayer and Bible reading works best. I want to be filled up and ready for the unexpected opportunities or crises I will face each day. I've also learned it's best not to check my emails or messages before my time with the Lord. I try to let Him be the one to set the course of my mind for the day.

It's true that our personal relationship with the Lord may be rich with feeling and deeply experiential in nature. But there's no getting around it. If we want to abide in Christ, we must build upon our relationship with Him day after day. As in any good relationship, this takes work.

Perhaps you're new to Bible study and prayer, or maybe you'd simply like a few practical tips in this area. In the next chapter I'll share the prayer method I've used for years, with some remarkable results.

Create Structure

Our spiritual house is vital. But our physical home is also important and requires planning and good management to function smoothly. The woman of valor in Proverbs 31 "watches over the affairs of her household and does not eat the bread of idleness" (verse 27). She gets up early, provides food for her family, and delegates tasks for her servants. Her family is clothed warmly so she's not afraid of cold weather (verses 15 and 21). And because of her expert home management, she "smiles at the future [knowing that she and her family are prepared]" (verse 25 AMP).

We look further and see that she adds to her family's wealth by expanding her trade. She is also kind and generous to the poor. All with a grace and dignity that earns the praise of her husband and children (verses 16-20,28). It makes me a little tired just to read about her. I'd like to think she didn't do all that at once, since most scholars believe we are probably glancing over the lifetime of a mature woman in these verses. But it's clear that hers was a well-run home that provided protection, structure, nurture, and even joy for her family.

All of us work at home whether or not we have outside employment. But it's also true that some women are naturally more talented at the creative and organizational aspects of a home. I have friends who create environments that are beautiful and inviting. They love to share their homes and serve others through their gifts of hospitality. They truly amaze me, because a well-ordered home doesn't come naturally for me. I'm still growing in this area—and probably always will be. But since home is important in caring for my family, I've devoted time and energy to learning how to create healthy meals, furnish and manage our household, establish good routines, and delegate chores.

Good management is vital to any home. A pastor friend who ministers among the poor tells me that *structure* is the first thing he introduces into their community. Other aspects of building strong families—like education, good health habits, financial management, good nutrition, and even Bible instruction—are more readily incorporated when there is a good structure at home.

When we fill our homes with good food, lovely furnishings, and peaceful surroundings, we are nurturing our families. A simple definition of nurture is "to help something or someone to grow, develop, or succeed; to take care of someone or something that is growing or developing by providing food, protection, a place to live, education."[9]

> When we fill our homes with good food, lovely furnishings, and peaceful surroundings, we are nurturing our families.

Nurture and *nourish* come from the same Latin word, so to nurture is to nourish. When we nurse a baby, or nurse a family member back to health, or even provide nursing care to a patient, we are both nourishing and nurturing.

Let's remember once again that the woman of valor is equal parts nurturer and warrior. We've seen how the warrior aspect was swept aside in Christian circles for years. But in today's world, it sometimes seems nurturing has been left in the dust of our ambitions. We must remind ourselves that to build wisely is to nurture. It takes time and patience to provide spiritual and physical nourishment for those we love. You can't rush growing things, and you can't shortchange nurturing if you want a healthy home.

Build a Strong Marriage

One of the nicest compliments I've ever received came from my own daughter, many years ago when she was a young teenager. We were headed somewhere in the car when Bethany turned to me and, out of the blue, said, "Mom, I want your life." She was talking about my life of shared ministry with David along with the challenge of caring for three active children. I was deeply touched, because this vibrant, talented, world-changer of a daughter of mine could have done anything with her life. And yet, she saw something in the often-messy workings of our family that made her want that life.

It's funny how things turn out, because many years later, that's exactly what she's doing. She and her husband have planted a church and are doing a wonderful job of raising their own little crew of four vibrant, active children. Maybe she's raising world-changers.

David and I are far from perfect, but we have placed our family as our highest priority, right after our relationship with the Lord. I'd like to think that our marriage and the way we raised the children set a good example. But mostly, I hope our kids felt loved. I agree with what David's dad told him before we got married. "Son," he said in his characteristically big, booming voice, "the best way to love the children you'll have one day is to love their mother." When he died, Dr. Howard Chadwick—our children's beloved "Granddaddy Chadwick"— had been a minister for more than 65 years. He and David's mom had been married almost that long when she died a few years earlier.

Granddaddy Chadwick's words still ring true. One of the best ways any of us can love our children is to build a strong marriage. Nothing else, in my opinion, can make a child feel more secure than two parents who are committed to each other through good times and hard times.

> To build a strong marriage is to build your house wisely.

A strong marriage brings health to your family. And when you grow strong faith by building your spiritual house, your chances of having a successful marriage increase dramatically. Studies have shown that in families where prayer and Bible reading take place, the divorce rate drops to less than 1 percent. To build a strong marriage is to build your house wisely.

Honor Your Husband

In looking further at the woman of valor, we see that "her husband is respected at the city gate, where he takes his seat among the elders of the land" (Proverbs 31:23). I love knowing my husband is honored by others. I've noticed that his honor somehow gives confidence to our children. What goes well with him spills over to the family.

David is not just my husband; he's my best friend. He is also the spiritual leader of our home. We don't always see eye to eye, but if we reach an impasse, I've learned to trust him. He's a very good leader. Do I sometimes have the better idea? Of course. So we have lots of give-and-take. Submission is often a nonissue for us because we're a good team. But God must have had a reason for telling me to support my husband's spiritual leadership (Ephesians 5:22-24). Giving David respect as leader has had a positive impact on our family. When I honor him, we're all made stronger.[10]

Honor seems to be a lost art in many marriages today. I'm not sure why, but I've noticed a growing disrespect in how wives talk to and about their husbands. One young friend told me she doesn't enjoy going out to lunch with her work associates anymore because she's grown tired of hearing them bash their husbands.

We see the woman of valor term, *eshet chayil,* used in another context, this time comparing her to a less honorable wife: "A wife with strength of character [woman of valor] is the crown of her husband, but the wife who disgraces him is like bone cancer" (Proverbs 12:4 NOG). Other versions say "decay" or "rot" in the bones. Dishonoring our husbands is a problem as old as time, and one that makes me want to shout, "Come on, girls, surely we're better than that!"

"Just Give Me a List"

After Bethany got married, she would sometimes call and say, "Mom, could you give me some tips?" She would ask for guidance on cooking, health, marriage, mothering, or whatever it was she needed to know more about. Then she'd add, "Just give me a *list*." Like her mother, the girl likes a list, so I'm sharing a few marriage tips. The list is always evolving, but David and I would agree that our number one tip—taking a day off together—has remained a constant throughout our marriage.

Mom's List of Marriage Tips

1. *Take a day off together every week:* For years, Friday has been our day off. We don't do work and rarely answer emails or phone calls. We enjoy a morning coffee, breakfast, followed by watching movies or whatever makes us feel rested. No wonder the Bible tells us to take a Sabbath. It's just plain good for us to unwind. It's fun and something we look forward to. The Sabbath was God's gift to humans and their families. There's a reason it's our favorite marriage tip.

2. *Pray for and with your husband:* Take time to pray alone and together. Develop your personal prayer life. But remember the power of agreement in prayer. Find Bible promises and stand on those together for your children. Studies show that marriages are stronger when couples pray. It's true; the family that prays together stays together.

3. *Dream big:* I agree with whoever said we are to dream dreams so big that only God can accomplish them. Our marriage grows stronger when we dream together rather than settling for a lesser life. Dreaming big for the miracle of children kept us going through years of infertility.

4. *Serve the less fortunate:* Explore ways to reach out to the poor. Travel to broken places in the world—especially with your children. This combats materialism better than lecturing your kids. Isaiah 58:8 is true. When you spend yourself on behalf of the hungry, your "healing will quickly

appear." Try tithing. Giving breaks the back of the "money monster" and helps you trust God.

5. *Take care of your temple:* You get only one body. The Bible calls it the temple of the Holy Spirit. Exercise. Eat healthy. Drink enough water. Little steps toward healthier living make a big difference. You'll improve your mental health and your marriage. Even anxiety and depression will lessen if you take better care of your "earth suit."

6. *Believe the best about each other:* Think about your spouse in a positive light. Marcus Buckingham, who wrote *The One Thing You Need to Know,* discovered the most common attribute in successful marriages is that spouses believe the best about each other. This would also be my top tip for raising children. Learn to see the beauty in those you love.

7. *Limit your possessions:* It's wonderful to enjoy God's good gifts. But be careful not to trust in material things or to let them control you. Be honest. Is enough really enough? Or do you demand excess? We're told not to trust in riches, and to be rich in good deeds (1 Timothy 6:17-18). A simple way to limit possessions is to limit the size of your home. One friend told me this was a life-changing insight for her.

Raising Strong Children

Our children used to have a running joke. When watching a lousy performer on *American Idol*—the kind who never made it past the first cut—they'd say, "Where *was* his mother?" Their point being that any good mom should never let her children go out into the world without a grasp of who they are and who they're not. What they're good at—and what they're not. It's our job as mothers to teach, nurture, and correct our kids. To tell them the truth about themselves and the world around them.

I've said that raising our children was my master passion, and it's true. Nothing has ever given me as much joy, as many tears, or greater triumphs than the development of these young people. Nothing I've accomplished compares with the exhilaration of pouring life into my kids and watching them flourish.

But being a mother has also been challenging. Even gut-wrenching at times. I once commented to an older, wiser friend who had raised five great kids that I wished I was a little more relaxed as a mom. She shot back, "Are you kidding? Motherhood is not a relaxing job!" And she's right. But with lots of prayer, hard work, creativity, patience, and a supportive "village," it can work.

The Heart of Childrearing

As I mentioned, prayer is vital to a good marriage. And praying for my children has been my "go to" method of childrearing. Pure and simple. This is more than just lip service, coming from a mom who knows she has plenty of flaws. I have often pored over God's Word to see what He had to say, and when I saw the Bible promised, "Their children will be mighty in the land" (Psalm 112:2), I figured I was on solid ground in praying they would have an impact on the world.

Surrender them to Christ is what I learned early on. Fight for them. Often it felt like war.

I also gave my best energy to developing their gifts and talents. In chapter 6, we'll explore ways to help our children realize their dreams. But at the heart of it all is prayer.

Study Your Child

I enjoyed looking for the potential in each of our children. Sometimes we're the only ones who truly see the beauty in our children. That's okay, because I believe God has given mothers special insight into their children's character and calling. We get to help them find their way in the world.

Well-known author and Christian psychologist, Dr. James Dobson, in *Hide or Seek*, emphasized the importance of helping our children develop a gift or a talent. We should also help our children look attractive, he said. Sound superficial? Think again. Reasonably stylish haircuts and clothing are not a waste, he argued. Having a talent along with an attractive appearance strengthens our children's self-esteem. They may be rejected for their Christian faith, he acknowledged, but not because they're simply out of step with the world.[11]

Answer Two Questions

Children are asking two questions: "Do you love me?" and "Can I have my own way?" Children seem to thrive on love and limits. We'd say, "Yes, I love you, and no, you can't always have your own way." Focused attention, eye contact, lots of snuggles, a listening ear—we have many ways to say "I love you." Limits are important too. Here's a little secret: If it's necessary to punish your children, give them punishments beneficial to them: early bedtime; cleaning the bathroom; reading a book instead of watching television; doing 50 jumping jacks to get the wiggles out. You get the point. I also learned as the boys hit middle school to go easier with eye contact. Chill out. Don't bear down too hard in conversations. That's probably why our best talks—especially the hard ones—happened while I was driving them somewhere. They'd tell me most anything I wanted to know if I didn't intrude into their lives.

> Focused attention, eye contact, lots of snuggles, a listening ear— we have many ways to say "I love you."

Include Them in Your Faith Journey

Faith is caught and taught. I encouraged our kids to be on the lookout for signs of God at work—in big ways and small ones.

> We dared our
> kids to dream
> big and trust
> God with
> the results.

Conversations in the van seemed to turn into spiritual lessons—I dubbed our drive time "e-van-gelism."

We dared our kids to dream big and trust God with the results. But mostly, I wanted them to be able to hear God—to discern His voice from all the others. They didn't know it, but I continually watched to see if their views were being shaped according to what they were learning at home or according to what the world was telling them.

We also tried to help our kids experience the laboratory of answered prayer. We included them in our faith journeys. When we were hoping for a third baby, we encouraged the older two kids to join us in prayer. It took three years of waiting, but they prayed relentlessly. So much that I finally told God I was going to be "really upset if You let these little kids down." And they were thrilled when their persistent prayers were answered!

The Power of a Safe Home

Every home needs love, freedom, grace, and structure to grow healthy families. Sometimes having a strong home can even be a matter of life and death. On a recent trip we made to Haiti, the head of Mission of Hope Haiti, an organization providing holistic care for families in impoverished villages, explained how a home is the difference between a safe child and a vulnerable one.

He showed us a hillside with two groups of homes, first pointing out row after row of blue tentlike structures that had been assembled as temporary housing after the devastating earthquake in 2010. Then he drew our attention to nearby rows of small but attractive cinder block homes constructed by his organization.[12] These homes were sturdy enough to withstand hurricanes, he told us. The roofs didn't leak, and they had a front door, which could be locked. Women and children living in them now felt safe.

And safety, he added quietly, is life-changing. Here's why: After the earthquake, the already impoverished Haitian villages were left even more vulnerable. The thousands of blue tentlike relief dwellings solved one problem but created another. Sexual predators could simply use a knife to slit the tents open and kidnap children. With communities in chaos, no one could control the abuse or abduction of these children, and Haiti became a hub for the sex trafficking of children.[13]

Mothers were constantly terrified for the safety of their little ones. So to move a woman and her family from a tent to a home with a door and a lock was the difference between daily panic and freedom. Mission of Hope calls the ministry of moving mothers from the blue tents to the cinder block homes "From Blue to Block."

It really doesn't matter where I travel. It's the same in any culture—rich or poor. We can never underestimate the power of a home. Home is where humans thrive and grow best. It's where children should be nurtured. Instructed. Protected. It's where they catch the faith. And where they're free to dream. Especially when the home is built on the solid rock of faith in Jesus Christ.

And when a woman of valor is both warrior and nurturer to her household, when she seeks the Lord with all her heart, when honor and respect are present, and when the marriage thrives, a home can produce children who are likely to change the world.

5

She Prays Hard

*[Anna] never left the temple but worshiped
night and day, fasting and praying.*

Luke 2:37

I still marvel when I think about the great faith of a young mother I met in a tiny country in a forgotten corner of the world. She was beautiful and graceful and looked to be in her mid-thirties. She was also a survivor of the horrific genocide in Burundi that had exploded alongside Rwanda's frenzy of killings in 1994. Those events sparked a brutal and exhausting civil war in Burundi that lasted over 12 years.

The war had recently ended, and I had been invited by African Leadership and Reconciliation Ministry (ALARM)[1] to teach a group of women on prayer. The couple of dozen women were church leaders and pastors' wives, and all had lived through the war. Their churches were working hard to bring healing and reconciliation to their nation. I looked around at the eager faces—these women were certainly no strangers to prayer or God's Word. I was impressed with their knowledge of the Bible. We wrapped up our lively discussion, and I asked if anyone wanted to share a personal story of answered prayer.

One woman told how God had miraculously kept her safe when her village was attacked. Another shared that with God's help, she had somehow managed to hide her brother when soldiers were furiously searching for him to kill him. Their stories were filled with victory and joy as they testified to God's faithfulness—even during times of scarcity and violence.

Finally, the lovely young mother I spoke of earlier rose to her feet and began to tell her story. She had eight children and lived in the nearby countryside. One day she was gathering vegetables when her children's caregiver rushed out with news that her two-year-old son had fallen ill. By the time she reached home, the child had died.

"I remembered the Bible story about how Elijah prayed for the widow's little boy who died," she said. "Elijah prayed and prayed and the boy finally came back to life. So I cried out, 'You did it for Elijah, Lord—do it for me!'" She told us she prayed and prayed for a long time—but, sadly, with no results. "Finally," she said quietly, "I could not bear to look at my son any longer, so I went outside to pray." She paused before going on with her story, as if uncertain how to continue.

I confess that by this point, I was already thinking about what I should say to her, about how we can look to God for comfort during those difficult times when it seems as though He has not answered our prayers. But I was not prepared for what happened next.

The young mom told us she went back inside the house to pray one last time. "But when I put my hands on my little boy's lifeless body and began to pray, he suddenly coughed and sputtered and sat up—he was alive!" An awe fell over the room, and there was a holiness about it all. There I was, face-to-face with an ordinary mother who lived oceans away from all that was familiar to me. But I knew I was in the presence of a true warrior and a woman of valor.

I hesitated about whether to share this story. You might be thinking, *Perhaps her little boy wasn't really dead.* Or *I wonder why God didn't heal my sick child.* A story like this raises many questions for which I don't have answers. But I do know this: God cares for His children all over the world. And in a place like Burundi—where they have tasted death up close and where doctors are nearly nonexistent—believers have experienced a dimension of God's grace I've not seen in my safe, suburban world.

> Miracles happen in the most broken of places.

I've heard similar stories firsthand from war refugees in Syria and slum dwellers in India. I'm always curious as to why God's people who have endured war and suffering—like this Burundi mom, like the women in Iraq, and like Esther—seem to possess such great faith. Greater than my own faith and greater than much of what I see in my corner of the world. Miracles like these sometimes happen in the most broken of places.

God does not love one group of people more than another. As Christians, we stand united on the unshakable truth that our salvation is only by God's grace, through faith, and that even that faith "is the gift of God" (Ephesians 2:8). The shed blood of Jesus—not miracles—is the proof of God's love.

But again, let's not lose sight of the fact that faith is a fight. Believing God's Word is sometimes a fierce struggle. Yes, faith comes by hearing God's Word (Romans 10:17). But we still must take time to fill our souls with the words of Scripture. Or as someone once put it, "Air is a gift, but we still have to breathe it."

I walked away from my encounter with this young mother awed, but also challenged. And while I realize God frequently doesn't heal or deliver or raise someone from the dead, I was inspired by the way she fought desperately for her child. She was persistent in prayer. She was courageous. And she went to war on behalf of her son.

This ordinary woman of valor has encouraged me not to be too quick to give up on God. Unlike the woman who recently said to me, "Oh, I prayed hard a couple of times for something I really wanted, and it didn't work. Guess I won't ever try *that* again."

At the very least, I want to look to God with a more expectant faith and to grow in my understanding of what it means to stand on His

Word. Scripture reminds us that the Word of the Lord endures forever (1 Peter 1:25). It's worth our best energy to read and study it. To fight the fight of faith. To believe it.

Take God at His Word

We've talked about the importance of building our faith, or our "spiritual house," upon our relationship with Jesus. The Bible tells us this "rock" is the only sure foundation upon which to build. Women of valor are both fighters and builders. Nurturers and warriors. But it's worth repeating: Training our hearts to hear God's voice is our most important task.

> Training our hearts to hear God's voice is our most important task.

The best way to learn how to hear the voice of God is to read His Word. It's that simple. The Bible helps us know God's promises, His great love for us, His plans, and His character. In short, the Bible helps us know God. But we must give Him time to speak to us. A few minutes each day to read and think about the promises in the Bible provides nourishment to our soul. It sharpens our "inner hearing" of God's voice. Jesus said, "My sheep listen to my voice; I know them, and they follow me" (John 10:27).

A woman of valor takes God at His Word. She believes what He tells her, even when everything around her looks impossible. Just think of Mary, the mother of Jesus. Her story started with a message from God delivered by way of a miracle—a visit from an archangel. Gabriel approached the young woman with the news that she had been chosen to bear the long-awaited Messiah!

She was incredulous and frightened. How could this be? She was a virgin. Gabriel comforted her and told her not to be afraid, for she had great favor with God. He reminded her that "nothing is impossible for God!" (Luke 1:37 CEV). Mary responded with these words of extraordinary faith and courage: "Let it be to me according to your word" (Luke

1:38 ESV). Her willing obedience resulted in a massive shift in the entire course of human history—all because a young woman of valor dared to take God at His word.

Pray and Walk Away

Sometimes I think back to that young mom in Burundi, and I wonder. Did Jesus marvel at her faith the way He marveled at the faith of the Roman centurion? I'd like to think so. The Bible tells us the soldier came to Jesus, desperate for his beloved servant who was paralyzed and suffering terribly.

> Jesus said to him, "Shall I come and heal him?" The centurion replied, "Lord, I do not deserve to have you come under my roof. But just say the word, and my servant will be healed. For I myself am a man under authority, with soldiers under me. I tell this one, 'Go,' and he goes; and that one, 'Come,' and he comes. I say to my servant, 'Do this,' and he does it." When Jesus heard this, he was amazed and said to those following him, "Truly I tell you, I have not found anyone in Israel with such great faith" (Matthew 8:7-10).

Jesus saw that the soldier was ready to walk away—in absolute trust—because he had grasped the fact that Jesus had authority to heal. Jesus marveled and told onlookers that He'd never encountered faith like that, even among the religious people. The centurion's servant was healed at that very moment.

As we learn to listen to the voice of God and take Him at His word, let's remember that, as women of valor, there are times to fight the fight of faith—to stand firm on God's promises. But there are also times when our boldest demonstration of faith is to be like the centurion and simply place our problem in the hands of Jesus, trusting Him to work. We pray and walk away.

The Secret Mailbox

"Friendship with God is reserved for those who reverence him. With them alone he shares the secrets of his promises" (Psalm 25:14 TLB). I love a good secret, don't you? Keeping a secret requires that we remain on our guard. We don't want to "spill the beans" in a thoughtless moment. The Bible says God has secrets, and He shares His secrets with His friends. Jesus said, "I have called you friends, for everything that I learned from my Father I have made known to you" (John 15:15). Prayer is kind of like keeping a secret with God. We take our secret requests to Him and remain alert to His voice, ready to take action as He leads.

> We take our secret requests to Him and remain alert to His voice, ready to take action as He leads.

When our children were small, I made up a game I called the "Secret Mailbox Club" to help them get a picture of what it means to entrust our secret hopes, dreams, and prayers into God's hands. I reminded them that when I put mail in our family's mailbox, I put the flag up and *walked away*. I didn't pitch a tent and wait anxiously for the mailman.

I encouraged the children to draw a picture of their heart's desire, a secret hope, a cherished dream. We put these "prayers" into our handmade construction paper mailbox and put the flag up. "Now let's trust God with our secret prayers," I'd tell them. "We can be sure He will send the answers in His way and in *His* time."

This little game helped them (and me) grasp the concept of trusting God and what it means to "cast" our cares on Him (1 Peter 5:7). If we truly trust in the character of our loving, all-powerful God, we can *pray and walk away* knowing that He knows what's best for us. Our hopes and dreams are now safely in His hands. And we'll rest secure as we wait for our "mail" to arrive.

Prayer Takes Practice

My husband, David, played basketball at the University of North Carolina for Dean Smith, one of college basketball's greatest coaches. One time David took our children to Chapel Hill to watch the team practice. He had to smile because Coach Smith ran practice exactly the same way he had when David played for him 20 years earlier.

Coach Smith would always tell his team that great players were made in practice, not in games. "You play like you practice." Coach's practice routine, along with a love for his players, earned him two NCAA championships, 11 Final Four appearances, and a long stretch as college basketball's all-time-winningest coach.[2] I guess it's true: If you find a way to practice that works, stick with it.

When it comes to prayer—like basketball—practice makes perfect. Jesus reminded us how important it is to hear and practice what we learn from Scripture: "Therefore everyone who hears these words of mine and puts them into practice is like a wise man who built his house on the rock" (Matthew 7:24).

Jesus simplified our practice of prayer by instructing us to abide in Him. "If you abide in me and my words abide in you, ask whatever you wish and it will be done for you" (John 15:7 MOUNCE). The word *meno*, translated *abide*, also means "to continue, to dwell, remain, rest, settle, to last, to endure, to survive, to permanent, and to wait for."[3] Abiding is continual. It's "pray[ing] without ceasing" (1 Thessalonians 5:17 ESV). Most importantly, it is a relationship. But like any good relationship, abiding takes work—and practice.

Years ago, I developed a simple prayer method that has remained a constant for me. I guess, like Coach Smith, I found a "practice pattern" that works. We talked earlier about the importance of creating structure in our households. I believe the same is true of our prayer lives. As women of valor, we should be continually finding ways to strengthen our faith.

Now, I'm not naturally drawn to a routine. The same is true with my prayer life. I admit that for years, my prayers were best fueled by a crisis. This was especially true during my years of infertility. A crisis makes me thirsty for God.

To some degree, that's true of most of us. But we can't create a spiritual life that's healthy if it is only energized by a crisis. People whose spiritual lives are forged from crisis to crisis seem to always be on the lookout for a new spiritual thrill. *This* miracle or *that* healing. This awesome worship song or that sermon—or the next *whatever*. You fill in the blank.

Many years ago, after the 9/11 attacks on our nation, I was inspired to amp up my prayer life. The threat of war jolted me into a more consistent pattern of prayer. I sensed God was calling me to pray strategically and expand the scope of my prayers to include specific people and even countries around the world.

I learned that daily abiding in Christ through a consistent pattern of prayer is important because we're not in a game; we're at war. Spiritual war. As soldiers and as women of valor, we need to be prepared.

What resulted was a series of rather dramatic answered prayers and life-changing encounters with people all over the world. For example, I ended up in the offices of two different African presidents, in Burundi and South Sudan, whose countries I had simply prayed for by name.[4]

Develop a Practice Pattern

These life-changing encounters were the result of praying more specifically, more deliberately. That's what establishing a pattern of prayer can do. A good prayer pattern puts it all together so we can abide in Christ continually. I begin each day with what I call my "morning launch." It looks something like this: I spend at least a half hour reading my Bible, allowing time for prayer, followed by a brisk half-hour jog. I like to say, "I don't eval-

> "I don't evaluate my day until I run, have my coffee, and pray."

uate my day until I run, have my coffee, and pray." I then build on the foundation of that morning launch by continuing my conversation with Jesus throughout the day—or abiding.

I encourage you to experiment to see what kind of pattern works for you. What time of day is best? Do you have a special place for your quiet time? Do you have a good Bible? (I always say the best translation is the one you will *read*.)

It helps to have a plan, which is why I'm going to share a few pointers from my prayer pattern with you. The method has remained pretty much the same because it works well for me. You can tweak it to suit your personality. One friend teasingly calls me her "prayer coach." Others have told me this format has been life-changing for them.

A prayer pattern is like any good practice. It makes us stronger. Lifts our mood. Helps us notice answers. It helps us abide throughout the day. Let's face it: Daily habits over time make us strong.

Keep Watch

If I had to choose one tip that has most transformed my prayer life, it's simply this: Be alert. In the Greek text, the word for "alert" can be translated *to keep watch*. Keeping watch can mean following Jesus's instructions to "watch and pray so that you will not fall into temptation" (Matthew 26:41). Or it can point us to the focused prayer life described in Colossians 4:2: "Devote yourselves to prayer, being watchful and thankful." Keeping watch is staying alert and watching for our enemy the devil, who prowls around looking for someone to devour (1 Peter 5:8).

John Wesley encouraged his followers to practice the "discipline of watching." And, of course, there's our Proverbs 31 woman of valor who "watches over the affairs of her household" (verse 27). There are endless ways to keep watch.

I like to think of keeping watch as my daily job description. Sounds simple, I know. But with way too much on my plate, keeping watch can get lost in the shuffle. I must be mindful. Nobody talks more than the Holy Spirit. No one acts with greater power. But am I watching for signs of God at work? Am I listening for His voice? I will blow right past God's answers if I am not watchful.

Looking back, things turned a corner when I began to take seriously this word of instruction: "You must be self-controlled and alert, to be able to pray" (1 Peter 4:7 GNT). Since praying with more alertness, I've noticed more answers. Are more of my prayers being answered or am I just more aware? I'm not sure. Either way, being alert and watchful has made my prayer life more rewarding. That means I'm more likely to stick with it—a good thing in and of itself.

What keeps you from being alert? Too much social media, food, television, or wine? Maybe you're just plain too busy. If you're serious about prayer, I encourage you to give some thought to de-cluttering your life. But first, ask yourself what gets in the way of prayer, and then answer honestly.

Take Aim

I added a detailed list to my rather free-flowing exercises in journaling. This helped me be more alert. A list helps me take aim when I ask and to pray more specifically. "You do not have because you do not ask God," the Bible tells us in James 4:2.

> Be specific enough in prayer to recognize the answer when it comes.

It's pretty hard to know whether our prayers are answered if we can't remember what we prayed for. A list helps us watch for answers. "In the morning, O Lord, You will hear my voice; in the morning I will order my prayer to You and eagerly watch" (Psalm 5:3 NASB). When the Bible talks here about "ordering" our prayers, it sure sounds like a list to me. How specific should we be when praying? I always say specific enough so that we recognize the answer when it comes.

Worry can energize our prayers. And we can learn to be more specific by channeling those worries into our prayer lists.

To make my list, I simply write down in my journal the people who are most dear to me. Then off the top, I list friends, coworkers, leaders, problems, hopes and dreams, areas of personal struggle...you name it. My list reflects the concerns on my heart. Your list will reflect yours. You may end up with as many as 50 items on your list.

I mentioned earlier that after the attacks on 9/11, I expanded the scope of my prayers. I prayerfully asked the Lord to put specific people and places on my heart. Those, too, made my list.

Then I simply number each item on my list from one to seven. I pray for all the number ones on Monday, twos on Tuesday, threes on Wednesday...you get the point.

Praying for all 50 concerns at one time would be daunting. But it's not hard to pray for around seven needs each day. I write the items on an index card. I especially like to use a simple wire-bound booklet of 3 x 5-inch cards, which I fondly refer to as my "Chubby Book." I have tried more sophisticated workbooks, formulas, even apps. Nothing works as well for my prayer list as the humble Chubby Book. We'll learn more about the Chubby Book in the next step.

The List
(here are a few examples from my list)

1. David
2. Bethany
3. DB [our son, David]

4. Michael

5. Mar

6. Ryan

7. Jessie

1. Cassie

2. India

3. Burundi

4. China

5. Lebanon

6. Iraq

7. Grandchildren

1. Extended family members

2. Children's teachers and coaches, etc.

3. Various other needs

Keep numbering one through seven until you have listed all the concerns on your heart. That way, if you end up with a long list, you can pray for just a few items each day of the week.

Use Your Sword

If you want to know God's will, read His Word. He will never communicate anything to you that contradicts His Word. God's Word, which is likened to a sword in Hebrews 4:12, helps us pray with authority. Use your sword.

> If you want to know God's will, read His Word.

Almost immediately after I went from being an unbeliever to a believer, I was stunned to realize the Bible made sense. The Holy Spirit is given to us when we accept Jesus. One of His roles is interpreter of God's Word.

The words of Scripture are mysteriously connected to Jesus Himself. I can't explain it, but John 1:14 tells us that He, the Word, "became flesh." The Greek word *logos* is translated *word* in the New Testament. It means "intelligence, or the expression of that intelligence."[5] *Logos* is the same word from which we get *logic*. If you want to know the mind of God and how He thinks, read His *logos*. You'll be reading His thoughts.

Reading the Bible daily helps us to be transformed by the renewing of our minds (Romans 12:2). I wouldn't have believed this to be true unless I had experienced, firsthand, the power of the Word to change my thinking, expose and heal areas of sin, conquer fears, give wisdom, and bring joy.

God's Word also empowers our prayers and aligns our requests with His will. That's why I like to combine prayer with reading the Bible—usually one chapter each morning. Then I meditate on what I call my "watchword." A watchword is simply the verse or two of Scripture from my daily reading that seems to speak directly to my heart—or maybe to a specific need that weighs me down. The Holy Spirit enlivens the very words of Scripture and helps them take root within me.

Here's where the humble Chubby Book comes in again: I simply write down my watchword from my Bible reading on a 3 x 5-inch card in my Chubby Book. I've already written the seven or so items from my prayer list on the adjoining card, as I mentioned earlier. Sometimes I use the watchword as a prayer or claim its specific promise for a person on my list. Other times I'll meditate on or memorize the verse. I especially like to take my sturdy little Chubby Book with me when I go for a walk.

Friends tell me this method of reading God's Word and praying for their "list" has simplified prayer and removed some of the burdensome nature from their quiet times. I even had a group of eighth graders tell me they love the Chubby Book method! For me, this method has brought joy, helped me notice answers to prayer, and has been easy to sustain over the years.

Gather Your Swarm

I recently heard about a group of schoolchildren who figured out a way to stop the bullying on their playground. Whenever a fellow student was being bullied, the other classmates would gather around the victim and simply stand without saying a word. This show of solidarity stopped the bullies dead in their tracks every time. The students nicknamed their tactic "the swarm."

As women of valor, we can learn a lesson from those schoolchildren. When we gather our "swarm" of prayer warriors in what the Bible calls the prayer of agreement, we can have a powerful impact in the spiritual realm.

Jesus was clear about the power of team prayer. He promised that when we are gathered in His name, even just two or three of us, He is right there with us. "Truly I tell you that if two of you on earth agree about anything they ask for, it will be done for them by my Father in heaven" (Matthew 18:19).

The Greek word translated *agree* is *symphone* (from which we get *symphony*), and means "together with the same voice." This word can also be translated *music*. I wonder if our prayers sound like music to God?

Let's remember that we saw Esther stick together with her swarm of believers to defeat Haman. There can be enormous power when you pray in agreement and read the Bible with your family. Do you have a prayer partner or take part in a small-group Bible study? Find ways to connect to a biblically based church. God never intended for us to live the Christian life alone. No soldier in his right mind would enter a battle without his comrades. Nor would a woman of valor. A swarm defeats bullies and wins wars.

Resist the Devil

Be armed and dangerous to the Enemy. I remind you of my favorite verse on spiritual warfare: "Submit to God. Resist the devil and he will flee from you" (James 4:7 NKJV). The "submitting to God" part must come first. We

> Our call is to fight the good fight with the right weapons.

could call this "the fear of the Lord," which we remember was the source of strength for our woman of valor (Proverbs 31:30).

Our call is to fight the good fight with the right weapons. We've talked a lot about spiritual warfare, and with good reason. We face a war on three fronts. We wrestle against the counter-biblical thinking of the world, the spiritual attacks of the devil, and the fallen flesh in which we live daily. Our arsenal of weapons, including God's Word and prayer, obedience, and good teammates, all help us fight on the first two battlefields.

But I haven't found a way to overcome the flesh except by hand-to-hand combat. Insisting that our flesh submit to God is a tough task. In fact, the Bible speaks of the crucifixion of the flesh. Paul tells us, "I strike a blow to my body and make it my slave" (1 Corinthians 9:27). Another version says, "I buffet my body [handle it roughly, discipline it by hardships] and subdue it" (AMPC). And don't forget that our Proverbs 31 woman of valor made her arms—and herself—strong.

That's another reason I'm such an advocate of physical exercise. For me, a good prayer pattern combined with regular exercise spills over into the other areas of my life. This routine helps me keep a rein on my flesh. The flesh could include any kind of physical or emotional impulse that leads us away from Christ. The Bible warns against "acts of the flesh" like fits of rage, hatred, envy; sexual immorality, drunkenness; and many more (Galatians 5:19-21).

I point you back to the temple upkeep section in my earlier list of marriage tips. The same principles apply here. See if your physical, emotional, and spiritual health improve. It's just plain common sense that when you're able to win battles with your flesh, you often keep the devil from taking advantage of your weaknesses.

A few practical reminders:

- Take your Chubby Book and go for a fast 30-minute walk. Pray, meditate, sing, memorize Scripture, and catch a little vitamin D all at one time. Try this five days a week for 30 days. That raises serotonin levels, so it's good for your mental health.

- Take a day off each week.

- Get enough sleep.

- Drink plenty of water and eat nutritious food.

- Stay faithful to your daily quiet time.

- Have a prayer partner who holds you accountable.

Be the Answer to Prayer

Being alert is my foremost tip for prayer. But answering God's call is where we bring it all home. What is God calling you to do? Try asking Him, "How should I pray? What can I give? Where should I go?" Listening to God's voice leads to practical action. Stepping out in faith always brings a blessing, as my friend Heather recently discovered when she and her husband, Shawn, adopted three children they'd been fostering. They already had two biological children, so overnight they became a family of seven. I'll let Heather share about what she experienced as she put her faith into action:

> Listening to God's voice leads to practical action.

Heather's Story

Choosing to trust God when He calls you to do something crazy and scary allows you to experience blessings you could never dream up on your own! Many days and nights, for weeks and months in our adoption journey, we found ourselves questioning whether we had heard God. We thought if we heard Him correctly, surely it wouldn't be so hard! We've since realized it was all part of His plan for us; to stretch us and prepare us for the joy to come—the joy that only He could see on the other side.

I used to struggle with anxiety and depression. At times, fear paralyzed me and held me back from so many things. I remember crying out to God, begging Him to heal me and rescue me from this mental prison. Because I knew He could.

But it wasn't until I felt Him call me to put my faith into action that I started to be free of the anxiety and fear. It started a few years ago when I was teaching the little kids one Sunday morning. I was talking to them about Joshua 1:9: "Be strong and courageous...for the Lord your God is with you wherever you go" [ESV]. I was really passionate and encouraging them to have no fear, because God was always with them, and so on. And as the words were coming out of my mouth, the Holy Spirit spoke to me and said, "Heather! Do *you* believe what you are telling them? You have these irrational fears about so many things. (One thing in particular was going on a mission trip.) Don't you *believe* that I will be with you wherever you go?"

I was floored. I immediately knew God was calling me to go on a mission trip, something I had feared for years and thought was only for "other people." People who loved to travel. Not me. But I knew I had to go! Put my faith into action and trust that God would be bigger than my fears. I took my first mission trip to the Dominican Republic. God gave me a peace beyond all understanding. While on the trip, I experienced such joy and peace and comfort in the presence of God because I was in the *will* of God! Now I go on a mission trip every year.

The same thing happened when God called us to adopt. Again, not something I naturally wanted or desired for my family, or even felt comfortable doing—in fact, it scared me to death. But because God called us to do it, we trusted Him and followed through in faith. And He has blessed our family in ways we never could have imagined. It is so comforting to know God is in control of our lives, and we are not. That is where the freedom truly comes to life for me.

These are a few of the ways you can develop a prayer pattern. As you establish yourself in prayer, you'll become more alert to seeing God at work in your life. Plus, you'll train your heart to listen. Spending time with God, as with anyone else, helps you grow more sensitive to His voice. It pays to be practical. To find ways to weave prayer into your daily life. You'll take the time to work hard at prayer only if you believe prayer really works—or that God works through your prayers. God loves it when you seek Him with your whole heart (Jeremiah 29:13). I encourage you to keep experimenting until you find the prayer pattern that works best for you.

Stand Together, Stand Strong

Guess why most missionaries leave the field. Not because of poor living conditions, a lack of creature comforts, or fear of threats like

Ebola or ISIS. Not rejection or attacks from the locals, and not even family issues. The reason most missionaries leave their assignment is conflict with other missionaries. I'd guess the same is true in churches. Internal conflicts in these places, like family conflicts, are the most destructive and painful of all.

Why do these stealth attacks happen so often? Mostly because they work. We are unaware and therefore don't guard against them. The devil is skilled at causing division. He did it with the angels. His name, *diabolos*, even means "divider." It's his job description. It's what he knows and loves best.

That's why, as women of valor, we need to be alert to the Enemy's tactics if we want to win our battles. We need to listen to God's voice. This means interacting with God through His Word and prayer. We must fight the right fight with the right weapons. And we need to stick together with other believers if we want to stand strong.

We can learn a lesson from the bottlenose dolphin. These extraordinary creatures can reason, solve problems, think abstractly, and even recognize themselves in a mirror! Dolphins can also swim up to 35 miles an hour. They're incredibly powerful and use their snouts as high-speed battering rams. No wonder they have virtually no natural predators.

As I mentioned before, my dad is a World War II submarine veteran. While on long, hot tours in the South China Sea, he and the other sailors hoped to see dolphins so they could dive off the sub for a refreshing swim—sure to be safe from sharks.

Sharks steer clear of dolphins for another reason: Dolphins don't travel alone. They find safety in numbers by sticking together in groups called "pods." Like dolphins, our teammates can help us stand against our enemies and gain strength in prayer.

Let's remember the prayer of agreement, or *symphone*, and how powerful our united prayers can be in battle. This principle was affirmed by a former Marine friend who saw combat duty in Iraq. "When danger hit," he explained, "I was trained to run toward the danger." His second response, he said, was to look around for his men. "So you could protect them?" I asked. "No," he said firmly. "I looked around for my men because I knew I couldn't do this mission by myself." Even the Marines know they need to stick together to stay strong.

As women of valor, our mission is too important and too dangerous to be accomplished alone. We have no control over how and when God chooses to answer our prayers. But what we can control is our commitment to be faithful in the daily process of prayer and studying and obeying God's Word. Fighting the fight of faith. Standing together with other believers. This is how we abide in Christ.

Let's dare to step out in faith and answer God's calling in our families, communities, and the world as an army—a swarm—of women of valor.

6

She Dares to Dream Big

*Her children rise up and call her blessed; her
husband also, and he praises her.*

PROVERBS 31:28 ESV

I can't believe how far I've come," said Shona as she prepared to enter her final year of medical school. Shona had gone to a high school where most kids didn't even graduate. She was the first in her family to attend college. Finally, she was almost a doctor!

I first met Shona when her ten-year-old brother played on our son's Amateur Athletic Union (AAU) basketball team. Shona was pretty, smart, and kind, but what really struck me was that she had taken a break from her own college studies to homeschool her younger brother. As a third grader, he struggled with reading, so Shona was determined to help him catch up. After five years of her diligent schooling, Shona's brother had not only become a strong student, but he was awarded the first full minority scholarship at a prestigious private school.

While taking the break from college, Shona also searched to find her own life's purpose. She volunteered at a group home that housed mentally challenged adults and worked at Hospice, which specializes in end-of-life care. "Those experiences sparked a fire in my heart," said Shona. "I wanted to go to medical school!"

"Getting back into college was not a problem," she told me. "Figuring out how to get into medical school was." Her guidance counselors were little help. "Maybe you should consider a small nursing program," they advised. "You're better suited to that." Medical schools are very selective, they told her, and only the highest quality students get in. "Maybe you should think about something more reasonable."

"At that point I became discouraged and began to consider alternative careers," she admitted. "That is, until my mother got wind of what was being told to me. I thought she would be understanding, but boy did she let me have it! 'Shona, don't you know *whose* you are? God is in control, not man. "Delight yourself in the LORD, and he will give you the desires of your heart."' Well, you can't argue with that, can you? I got into medical school."

Even while in medical school, Shona helped other kids to keep working toward their goals. Her supervisor once wrote, "Every weekend, while most students were studying for tests, Shona drove several hours to teach SAT prep classes to poverty-level kids at her church, making her high grades even more impressive. Shona was one of the most talented and dedicated students in the program. She will make a knowledgeable, kind physician."

Today Shona is a family medicine physician with a family of her own. She serves her community and still loves to give hope to kids, inspiring them to realize their own dreams.

> Some of her fiercest battles are when she fights for her dreams—and for the dreams of those she loves.

Both Shona and her mother are women of valor who dared to dream big. Their dreams took plenty of faith, courage, and persistent prayer—especially when going against the grain of a community where some had lost their ability to dream.

God Is the Dream-Giver

A woman of valor is brave in the face of life's battles. She knows what it means to fight for her faith, her family, and her community. Some of her fiercest battles are when she fights for her dreams—and for the dreams of those she loves.

It's been said we grow great by our dreams. Perhaps that's because most dreams don't come without a fight. A woman must have the courage to dream big. Especially in today's world, where some believe dreams are impossible to achieve. Young people have confided they don't want to dream big for fear of disappointment. How tragic.

It is hard to dream big. Dreams take more than courage. Dreams take creativity; dreams take work; dreams take self-sacrifice; dreams expose us to pain and disappointment; dreams take persistence; dreams require that we sometimes stand alone. It's no wonder dreaming big can drive us a little crazy.

I have to tell you a secret. Even during those years when I didn't believe in God, I prayed something like this: "God, I don't believe You are real, but if You ever show me You exist, which I seriously doubt, I will believe in You." Deep down inside, I feared that if there was a God, He could not be trusted with my dreams.

I suspected God was something of a dream-killer instead of the wonderful Father who planted those dreams in my heart. Later, after I

> God is the Dream-Giver.

received Jesus as my Savior, I learned that not only can God be trusted with my dreams, but His plans for my life were far better and more exciting than my dreams. Far from being a dream-killer, God is the Dream-Giver.

I've also learned that God is creative and made each of us for a different purpose. It's worth our best efforts to seek Him wholeheartedly and answer the unique calling He has on our lives. Most people want to believe their life on earth can make a difference.

Even children long to know their purpose. Earlier I mentioned my husband's father, the late Dr. Howard Chadwick. He used to encourage our three children to search for their life's calling. "Look around you at the needs you see in the world," he would tell them. "Then take an honest look at your own gifts and talents. Your calling may be found where the two intersect." Though he is no longer with us, we still refer to "Granddaddy Chadwick's rule" for discovering your life's mission.

How exciting to realize we are "God's masterpiece" and that "He has created us anew in Christ Jesus, so we can do the good things he planned for us long ago" (Ephesians 2:10 NLT). It makes sense that He would hardwire into each of us the necessary combination of gifts and life experiences to enable us to fulfill our calling. Friend, it's my prayer that as we continue to explore what it means to be a woman of valor, you'll discover the work God has planned just for you.

Her Children Rise Up!

When I first began to learn about the woman of valor, I asked David how he saw me as a fighter. He didn't hesitate to answer, "You have fought for our children's dreams." In thinking more about his comment, I realized I've fought harder to help our kids achieve their dreams than I ever fought for my own. Not that I didn't love setting goals and working hard to reach my dreams. I still do. But this quote says it best: "Reaching your own dreams is fulfilling—helping someone else reach their dreams is sublime." And when that "someone else" happens to be your own children, it's like joy on steroids.

I wonder if the Proverbs 31 woman of valor discovered this same joy in seeing her children realize their dreams. We're told, "Her children rise up and call her blessed" (verse 28 ESV). Most likely, the children were older when they praised her in this way. I'd like to think they were now grown, happy, and fulfilled. They had achieved their dreams, in large part, because of their mother's faithful nurture and instruction in their home. Children generally won't praise their mother if their own lives are a wreck. It's the successful athlete we see on the television screen mouthing the words, "I love you, Mom." Not the prisoner on death row.

The Hebrew word translated *rise up* is a strong expression (verse 28). There's more to it than simply standing to one's feet. The word can mean "to accomplish, to endure, to build or establish, to strengthen, to succeed."[1]

Nothing makes me happier than when my children "rise up" and succeed. If the Proverbs 31 woman of valor poured her life into raising her children, as the chapter suggests, then I can imagine her joy as she watched them flourish. She had taught them diligently. Nurtured, clothed, and cared for them. She modeled a life of giving to the poor. She displayed joy, faithfulness, and laughter. Perhaps they saw their mom in prayer, seeking the Lord and fighting for their dreams. She gave her life to them.

To love our own children, and other children who are like our own, calls for self-sacrifice. But we may discover that loving others more than we love ourselves can be oddly liberating. The best mothers I know are passionate about seeing their children thrive—often putting their children's needs above their own.

One of the questions I'm most often asked is, "How do I help my children reach their dreams?" This question seems to go hand in hand with another one I've also been asked: "How do I make my own dreams come true?"

Over the years, I've learned the same principles hold true for both. We'll talk more about reaching our own dreams. But first, I want to share some tips I've learned about helping our children reach their dreams. And my fervent hope is that these principles will apply to your dreams as well, and help you to "dream big."

How to Help Your Children Reach Their Dreams

Learn to See Your Child's Beauty

> *By faith Moses, when he was born, was hidden for three months by his parents, because they saw that the child was beautiful, and they were not afraid of the king's edict* (Hebrews 11:23 ESV).

Seeing our children's beauty takes spiritual insight. Moses's parents saw he was a "beautiful child." The word translated *beautiful* in Hebrews 11:23 is used only one time in the entire New Testament. It means "urbane, refined, and a city dweller."[2] His mother and father risked their lives to hide Moses from the king's genocidal plot for three months. In that short time, they observed his unique beauty. Perhaps they sensed that he would be well-suited to be educated in the sophistication of Pharaoh's courts. It wasn't by accident that Moses's mother— a courageous woman of valor—placed him in a basket on the riverbank where she knew Pharaoh's daughter would find him. Moses would go on to lead God's people out of captivity in Egypt.

> God's dreams for your children often unfold as you learn to see their beauty.

God's dreams for your children often unfold as you learn to see their beauty. This points us back to the earlier emphasis on studying your child in chapter 4. I encourage you to pray for insight into their talents, gifts, and character.

I'll say it again: Sometimes mothers are the only ones who can see the beauty in their children's souls. God gives parents that special gift. That's why we're their best advocates.

I chose to be home with our children when they were young. Not because I was afraid they couldn't make it without me, but because my goal was to raise world-changers. For me, being a stay-at-home mother was the best way to achieve that goal.

Discovering the beauty in our children was, for me, the most intriguing aspect of parenting. But it took time and energy…and lots of watching. I also wanted to be the one to help launch their dreams.

Grow Your Child with the Grain

> *Train up a child in the way he should go [and in keeping with his individual gift or bent], and when he is old he will not depart from it* (Proverbs 22:6 AMPC).

Education should be a delight, not drudgery. It's the same with spiritual training. Children learn differently. Research has shown that some of what were previously thought to be learning disabilities are often different ways of processing information. The Lord of the universe seems never to tire of creating unique humans. At birth, every person is "wired" differently from the other people on the planet (7.4 billion at this writing)—and from every other person who has ever lived. Astounding, isn't it?

So as parents, it makes sense that in addition to discovering our child's unique beauty, we should experiment to see how they best learn. What makes them tick. The kindest way to raise our children is "in keeping with their gift or bent." Our best clues come simply from watching what they naturally love to do.

Our three children were all very different as they grew. Bethany was multitalented and loved to learn. She played volleyball and basketball, but she was also passionate about languages. In third grade she chose to attend a French Immersion Magnet School where English wasn't even spoken. She learned everything from English grammar to long division *in French*. It's easy to see why she now loves educating her children at home.

David, our older son whom we call DB, was shooting wads of trash through lampshades at age two. It's no surprise that basketball grabbed his heart at an early age. Basketball scholarships completely paid for both his undergraduate and master's degrees. We've watched basketball, along with his good math mind and strategic business acumen, open doors to his career path in the sports world.

Our youngest, Michael, was talented in a variety of sports, but gravitated to swimming and carved his own unique trail as a world-class collegiate swimmer. Our determined Michael likes to say, "Swimming found me!" His athletic gifts and work ethic, combined with his high "EQ," or emotional intelligence, have made him an effective leader, especially as his college swim team's captain.

David and I tried to grow our three children "with their grain." By God's grace, as they've grown older, they've not left the foundation of that training or their faith in Christ.

Challenge Your Child to Dream Big

> Blessed are those who fear the LORD... Their children will be mighty in the land; the generation of the upright will be blessed (Psalm 112:1-2).

Since they were born, I've prayed our children would be "mighty in the land." God created us to dream and placed the seeds of those dreams in our hearts—even as children. Our children are who they are, in large part because they followed the path of their dreams. I noticed over the years that around age ten, something of a lifelong dream began to emerge. Other parents have told me they noticed the same thing with their children.

> God created us to dream and placed the seeds of those dreams in our hearts.

We took those early childhood dreams seriously. David and I tried to identify, invest in, and protect them. We believed the dreams could be the pathway to God's destiny for our children. After all, He's the one who gave them the gifts and talents to reach their dreams. One of the greatest gifts you can give your children is to believe in their dreams and invest whatever you can in the development of those dreams.

Dreaming is as natural as breathing for children. What's not so natural is the self-discipline it takes to reach their dreams. David and I helped our kids experiment until they found something they loved and were good at. Then we'd provide structure and discipline to help them stick with it for a mutually agreed-upon length of time. At least until their efforts brought some measure of success.

For example, our children loved sports. But at different times, each would have chosen to skip out on practice, especially those grueling early-morning workouts. That's when our role was to provide that little extra push to get up early. As they got older and developed a passion for their dreams, their own self-discipline kicked in with a fierce determination. Dreams energize effort. And over time we saw how small but faithful habits helped our children accomplish those dreams.

Teach Your Child to Work Hard

Whatever you do, work at it with all your heart, as working for the Lord, not for human masters (Colossians 3:23).

I've had to learn some parenting lessons the hard way. I am not a naturally self-disciplined person. But I discovered early on that it was nearly impossible for me to take the kids beyond where I had gone myself. If I was undisciplined, it was hard to discipline them. If my schedule was inconsistent, it was hard to help them follow a schedule. If I quit before I reached the finish line, it was hard to teach them to persevere.

When an airplane loses cabin pressure, we're told to administer oxygen to ourselves before we give it to our children. We must "administer to ourselves" some lessons before we can teach them to our children. Hard work is one of those.

We encouraged our children to see all work as honorable—whether waiting on tables, doing weekly chores, or even folding laundry. Sometimes I would point out those who appeared to be "working with all their heart," like the guy who loaded up our groceries with an especially cheerful attitude. Hard work is vastly underrated in today's culture. It's important to talk about the importance of big dreams. But without plenty of hard work, they remain just dreams.

Build a Team Around Your Child

Let us consider [thoughtfully] how we may encourage one another to love and to do good deeds (Hebrews 10:24 AMP).

Every dreamer needs a team. Build a good team around your child. Bring teachers, grandparents, coaches, and church leaders into your circle of friends. They can be some of your biggest allies in helping your children reach their dreams. Prayer partners are also key, along with the parents of your children's friends. It really does take a village.

I supported our children's teachers and coaches and volunteered whenever possible. Coming from a family of educators, I deeply admired the many adults who poured their lives into our children. I prayed for them, encouraged them, even befriended them.

But sometimes I had to go to bat for our children. On a couple of occasions, I asked a teacher or coach to consider giving a second chance or a harder challenge to one of our children. In each case, I knew the child was ready. And in each case, the teacher or coach agreed, so I was glad I spoke up.

I want to add a brief word here about the people I call dream-killers. David and I have been more intentional about protecting our children against dream-killers than we have protecting them against drugs. Children usually recognize the stupidity of drugs, but they may not always see the subtlety of a dream-killer. Dream-killers can come in the form of peers or even adults at times. This is sometimes called "the crab-pot syndrome." When one crab tries to crawl out of a pot, the others will pull him back down. Not everyone sees our children's dreams as clearly as we can.

Again, that's why we have prayed fervently for God to guard our children's dreams. To use those dreams to draw our children close to Him, and then to open doors for their calling to make an impact for Christ on this broken and hurting world.

Serve with Your Child

If you spend yourselves in behalf of the hungry and satisfy the needs of the oppressed, then your light will rise in the darkness, and your night will become like the noonday (Isaiah 58:10).

Whenever possible, David and I included our children in serving others. When Michael was around eight, I took him with me to work with some moms and children from a fragile community who were being served by our church. One little boy, also named Michael, had to be carried around by an adult. Our Michael wondered how he could help. The program director told Michael the little boy simply needed a special kind of orthopedic crutches so he could walk on his own.

Michael persisted until I called our orthopedic doctor friend, who just "happened" to have some of those very crutches available. Michael made sure the other little Michael received a pair. I told him the little boy's mom had been praying for some crutches for her son. To which Michael replied, "Cool…I answered a prayer." I agree. It is very cool to find ways we can be the answer to someone else's prayer.

I keep saying the same thing again and again, but with good reason. As women of valor, we find life as we give our lives away to others. From my experience, helping our children understand that concept is also one of the greatest gifts we can give them.

Encourage Your Child to Listen to God's Voice

My sheep listen to my voice; I know them, and they follow me (John 10:27).

> Train your children to hear God's voice.

Train your children to hear God's voice. Find creative ways to teach them God's Word. But remember, although songs and memory verses are great, kids also need to learn how to apply biblical principles to the problems they encounter in the world. Toss out opportunities for them to think biblically. This will also help them listen for God's calling on their lives—their dreams.

An astute older friend, whose children were grown, once gave me some advice I have always taken to heart—especially since our children, like hers, went to secular schools. "I helped my kindergartners deal with the problems they faced on a kindergarten level. Then each successive year, I taught them to look at life from a biblical worldview for that age level. By the time they were in high school, they were well practiced at confronting a secular worldview." And, I would add, our children learned to see the people around them who did not believe in Jesus as friends to be won for Christ. Not enemies to be avoided.

I felt comfortable with our children being out in the world once I sensed they had learned to hear God's voice for themselves. They accepted Jesus at an early age and were learning how to apply God's truth. Plus, I was involved in their schools and their friendships, and set clear boundaries. At times, our rules were stricter than those of their friends—and that was okay.

As I mentioned earlier, we included our children in our own faith walk. We encouraged them to pray for some of the issues we faced as a family. Children are realists. They pray in specifics and notice when prayers are answered. They're also honest about the pain of unanswered prayers. Jesus loved children for lots of reasons, including their unfiltered honesty. And as Anna Grace, our oldest grandchild, once reminded me, "Jesus loves children because we are so fun to play with!"

Train Yourself to Sustain Yourself

Let us throw off everything that hinders and the sin that so easily entangles. And let us run with perseverance the race marked out for us (Hebrews 12:1).

I want to encourage you as a parent to take care of yourself. This goes back to our earlier discussion about building your spiritual house. Your relationship with Jesus is the foundation. Your marriage is next. Children love knowing their parents have a healthy marriage. And that they are strong as individuals. Your strength in the home will set a climate that somehow encourages your children to dream big.

> Your strength in the home will set a climate that encourages your children to dream big.

Mothering is a marathon, not a sprint. Pace yourself. Are you taking care of your "temple"? Getting enough exercise, good food, pure water? Do you have good friendships? Prayer partners? Now I sound like a mother, don't I? But it's so important for us, as moms, to guard our mental and emotional health. Malachi 2 warns us to guard ourselves in the spirit as a protection against the breaking faith that is divorce (verses 15-16).

So "throw off everything that hinders and the sin that so easily entangles" as Hebrews 12:1 encourages. Be alert and watchful for the purpose of prayer (1 Peter 4:7). One of our children once asked me, "Mom, do you enjoy us?" Wow. I had to pause and reflect. And I became more mindful to enjoy my children and our family, rather than merely "enduring" them. A thankful heart is a happy heart and makes for a happy home where children, and their dreams, can grow tall.

Fight for Your Dreams

I don't believe our God-given dreams, or the dreams of our children, can become realities without prayer. Earlier we talked about how to harness the energy of worry for prayer. Our dreams are another good way to energize our prayers.

I've shared some ways we tried to help our children reach their dreams. And again, these same principles apply to our own dreams. Dreams are fragile in so many ways. It doesn't take much to throw water on them—especially in children. Dreams can be broken by peers who reject and ridicule; by loss, by divorce, by prejudice, by circumstances; by illness or sin; by robbery, war, or poverty. That's why, when people ask me, "How do I make my own dreams come true?" I always add this to my answer: "Draw close to God and seek His calling on your life. Then get ready to fight fiercely for the dreams He gives you."

Perhaps you have only tiny fragments left of dreams that were shattered somewhere in your life. Maybe you gave up hope long ago. Or maybe you found a way to numb out or cover up your loss. You may have found better dreams and moved on. Or you might be saying, "No, it's too painful to dream. I'll take the path of least resistance."

Friend, is even a flicker of your dream still burning in your soul? I pray that at this moment, as you read these words, the Lord will begin to breathe life back into your broken dreams. Broken dreams can leave people vulnerable. Some find that when their dreams were gone, so was their life plan—and they lost focus. Especially in fragile communities, children trying to climb out of their environment to reach their dreams often are pulled back in by the "gang." Without meaning to, dreamers are often a threat to those around them who have forgotten how to dream.

Dreams are not simply an add-on. They help us stay on track with God's plans for our lives. They give us energy and motivation. They're cause for great joy and celebration. "When the LORD restored the fortunes of Zion, we were like those who dreamed. Our mouths were filled with laughter, our tongues with songs of joy. Then it was said among the nations, 'The LORD has done great things for them.' The LORD has done great things for us, and we are filled with joy" (Psalm 126:1-3).

> Dream dreams so big only God can accomplish them.

I want to encourage you to dream dreams so big only God can accomplish them. And to dare to be so specific that you can take a small step today to follow those dreams. I can hear the arguments:

"In this economy? I don't have the money."

"I'm only a wife and mom. What other talents or skills do I have?"

"There's too much to do, too much responsibility. Just ensuring my family is cared for is hard enough."

"I've waited too long. My dreams will never happen."

My favorite spiritual warfare verse also applies to dreaming big: "Submit to God. Resist the devil and he will flee from you" (James 4:7 NKJV). Dear friend, with God's help and by placing yourself firmly in His care, it's time to dream big again—but this time, keep the devil from stealing your dreams.

Do You Have Something the Devil Wants?

We often encounter stubborn resistance when trying to reach our God-given dreams. Could it be that some battles are harder than others because the Enemy knows the stakes are so high?

The answer to that thought came clear to me in a parking lot, of all places. I was heading home after a quick run for coffee with my husband. From a distance, we saw what appeared to be an aggressive bird battle under some nearby cedar trees. As we got closer, we saw the target of this assault was a large hawk. His noisy attackers were about half a dozen black crows. The angry birds darted in and out, fiercely attacking the hawk.

Now, I'm no bird expert, but I have heard hawks can slice the eyes of their opponents with one swipe of their razor-sharp talons. I, for one, would never mess with a hawk. What motivated a bunch of pesky crows to be so reckless?

Looking closer, I realized the hawk had some kind of rodent in his clutches. The hawk's "hands were tied," so he couldn't defend himself. The black birds were daring and relentless. Not to be outwitted, the hawk suddenly swooped up and sought refuge in the dense and prickly branches of a nearby cedar, where he was finally able to enjoy his lunch.

What's the point? Those crows didn't attack the hawk just for sport. That hawk had something the crows wanted—a nice meal in the form of a freshly caught animal. Predators come after their victims because they want what their victim has.

Perhaps you feel as if you've been fighting unseen enemies that come at you from all sides like a pack of crows. The battle has been fierce. Your foes are relentless. My question for you is simply this: What do you have that the devil wants? Perhaps he wants to steal your dream. Even a dream that seems ordinary can have a far-reaching impact. The Enemy doesn't know your future, but he sniffs out your destiny just like those crows sniffed out the hawk's catch.

I think back to our long years of infertility and the fierce fight to have a baby. I couldn't have known it at the time, but I was waging a battle not just for our firstborn, a daughter, but also for our next baby, a son. Then another son. Then four grandchildren and counting.

As our daughter once said to me, "Mama, you didn't know when you were going through all those years of infertility that you were fighting for all these people to be born." My fight was fierce because the Enemy wanted what I had—the promise of children and grandchildren who would glorify God. And ultimately, generations beyond those.

But friend, I had something else the Enemy wanted. And so do you. He wanted to steal my testimony. He wanted to make it impossible for me to tell the miraculous story of God's healing that enabled me to have those babies. He wanted to rob me of the chance to encourage others who are waiting for answers to their own prayers.

Quite simply, the devil wants to steal the story God is weaving through your dream. Or through this trial you're enduring so bravely. He wants to steal your testimony. In the end, he wants to steal God's glory.

> One day you will have a story to tell that will bring God much glory.

I encourage you to take a lesson from the hawk. Stand your ground. Hold on to your dream. Keep fighting and praying. Most importantly, seek refuge in God's strong love just like that hawk found safety in the cedar. And don't give up. God is faithful. One day you will have a story to tell that will bring Him much glory.

Help Others Dream Big

If you are around me for very long, you'll know I talk a lot about dreams. I suppose I have always been a bit of a dreamer, and for that reason I still can't seem to resist an adventure. My kids knew that full well growing up. We'd be traveling somewhere, and then Mom would unexpectedly turn off on some side road just to see what was at the end of that interesting rabbit trail. "Another one of Mom's adventures," they'd call it. Once I heard the youngest remark to his brother in the backseat of our van, "One day that woman's gonna get herself killed."

Well, I didn't get myself killed. But following God's sense of calling over the years has taken me to some pretty amazing places. The sense of adventure God placed in my heart has opened doors for me to see His work on six continents, where I've worked to help others reach their dreams. But there's more to this work than simply a motivation to do good.

> Fighting for the dreams of others is a remarkably effective form of self-help.

I've shared how the years of infertility brought me to my knees, especially when my own dreams for having children looked shattered and hopeless. Those years of waiting taught me a few things about holding on to dreams. I learned some secrets about waiting that are a valuable part of my life to this day. Each time I lose hope in a dream of my own, each time I want to give up, I've learned to step out of my pain and try to help someone else hold on to their hope. God's odd economy is once again proven true: We find life as we give our lives away. Fighting for the dreams of others is a remarkably effective form of self-help.

Become a Mother in Your Community

Deborah was a mother in Israel. In Africa, all women are called mothers. Will you dare to be a passionate mother and woman of valor in your own home? Will you learn to see the beauty in other children in your neighborhood? In your community? Maybe you're called to be a mom to someone else's kids who are fighting for their dreams. Just love them like they're your own.

I'm inspired by a friend who started a school among the poor in Brazil. She has noticed a remarkable cause for hope. A child may live in the *favela*, or "slum," she said. But if you can help him or her to accept Jesus and also provide a good education, the child begins to dream big. Then, miraculously, the favela begins to leave the heart of the child even before the child is able to leave the favela. She has witnessed this transformation with many children from the favela who work hard and reach their dreams.

> The next generation is desperate for women of valor to help them fight for their dreams.

The next generation is desperate for women of valor to help them fight for their dreams. Whether or not you have children of your own, some child somewhere needs you. Let the Lord speak to your heart. First, pray for your own children to be "mighty in the land" (Psalm 112:2). Then pray for the children in other communities to rise up too. Ask the Lord, "How should I pray? Is there something I can give? Where are You calling me to go?"

Perhaps, while reading this book, you've been reflecting on whether there is a holy discontent, an injustice, that burdens your heart. Or maybe you prayed that dangerous prayer, "Lord, break my heart for what breaks Yours."

I've sensed that today's women are growing more and more restless. I've never seen a generation more passionate, teachable, and eager to live large for God than this one. They're looking for clarity and support. They want to be strong women at home for their own families. And they're also looking for the courage to step out of their places of comfort and make a difference in the world around them.

Whether you're a young woman eager for encouragement, or you're older and more experienced (with years of wisdom to pour into someone else), the Lord is calling you to dream big.

> Doesn't it make your heart beat a little faster to realize that God has called us to be women of valor at this very time in history?

You can begin by asking yourself some questions: What are my gifts and talents? What do I love to do? How has God uniquely gifted me for a purpose? Where does He need me most? How can I begin right now to make myself strong for the task ahead of me?

There's plenty of talk these days about all the problems facing our families and our communities. Yes, our times are turbulent. But doesn't it make your heart beat a little faster to realize that God has called us to be women of valor at this very time in history? Let's dare to dream big, and then be willing to jump into the fray to make a difference in our broken and hurting world.

7

She Leads with Kindness

The teaching of kindness is on her tongue.

PROVERBS 31:26 ESV

Disney got it right. The scariest villains are often women. Think about it. Cinderella's wicked stepmother overworked the poor girl and locked her in an attic before she finally met her prince. The evil Maleficent cast her jealous spell on Sleeping Beauty. Snow White battled a wicked queen who was envious of her beauty. And don't forget Cruella de Vil ("cruel devil"), who kidnapped an entire litter of Dalmatian puppies, intending to use their fur to make coats.

The brothers Grimm capitalized on the sinister female. In their retelling of an old German fairy tale, a young brother and sister are captured by a cannibalistic witch who lives deep in the forest. She lures them into her house made of gingerbread and candy. The two children eventually manage to destroy the witch and escape—giving us a happy ending to the story of Hansel and Gretel.

Jacob and Wilhelm Grimm, whose fairy tales had to be sanitized before they were suitable for children, were said to have portrayed a few mothers as villains. But the public outcry against the idea of mothers mistreating their own children forced the brothers to recast the mothers as evil *stepmothers* instead.

When I was a small child, the wicked woman that terrified me most—hands down—was the Wicked Witch of the West in the movie *The Wizard of Oz*. All these years later, I can still hear that green-faced old witch cackling "my pretty" as she taunts her captive, Dorothy.

A woman devoid of what Shakespeare called "the milk of human kindness" is a fearsome creature—especially to a child. Maybe that's because as children, we instinctively open our hearts to women. From birth, we're trained to look to our mothers for nurture and protection.

> Kindness is central to the character of any woman of valor.

That's why it's vital that we learn to balance our nurturer and warrior roles. When we do that, the people around us flourish. We have explored what can happen when the warrior side, or the "fight," is taken out of a woman—how she and those in her care are left vulnerable. In this chapter we'll take another look at the equally damaging results that can occur when a woman's nurturer side is stolen from her.

Kindness is central to the character of any woman of valor. "She opens her mouth with wisdom, and the teaching of kindness is on her tongue" (Proverbs 31:26 ESV). A woman of valor is not only kind; she "teaches others to be kind" (verse 26 ICB).

The simple dictionary definition of *kindness* points to words such as "gentle, considerate, or friendly." But the Bible gives kindness a much stronger meaning. It is listed among the fruit of the Holy Spirit present in the life of a believer (Galatians 5:22). The word *chrestos*, translated as *kindness*, is described as a "grace that pervades one's whole nature" and is the opposite of harshness or severity. Christ's yoke, or what He asks us to do, is *chrestos*, having nothing harsh or galling about it (Matthew 11:30).[1]

As we continue to look at the full portrait of the Proverbs 31 woman, we'll see her kindness only adds to her strength. She is both leader and teacher. She speaks words of wise instruction to her family and others. But her leadership is always wrapped in kindness.

Let's remember that God created us to be both strong and kind—part warrior and part nurturer. We talked earlier about how, in the very beginning, He designed woman to be the helper, or *ezer*—a source of rock-like support for her husband (Genesis 2:18). God has equipped us, as *ezers*, with courage and strength. But He added to our strength by making us capable of being kind and nurturing.

I still marvel when I think about how God gave us, as women, the added privilege of being life-givers and cocreators of the entire human race. Eve was the first woman. Her name literally means "mother of all the living" (Genesis 3:20). I love Eve's response after giving birth to the first human ever born to a woman: "Look, I have created a new human, a male child, with the help of the Eternal" (Genesis 4:1 THE VOICE). Another translation puts it this way: "I produced a man..." (TLV).

We're not only able to bear children, but also to nurture them. What's more, we have the ability to nurture children not necessarily our own. We'll see that played out when we look at Deborah, the prophet, judge, and "mother in Israel." Throughout Scripture, we find examples of this beautiful nurturer and warrior combination that God has mysteriously woven into the heart of a woman.

But the Bible also warns us of the "enmity," or hostility, between Satan and the woman after the fall (Genesis 3:15). It makes sense, then, that the devil would try to lure the woman away from God's original design, twisting her *ezer* strength into a rock—not of support, but of hardness. Distorting her courage into brazen ambition. And if he can derail her nurturer side—killing the kindness in a woman's heart—he will have unleashed a creature who is destructive to her family, to the culture around her, and ultimately to herself.

Our Own Worst Enemy

The hostility between Satan and women has played out again and again on the stage of human history. Wherever we see women being mistreated, we can be sure the devil is lurking behind the scenes, manipulating others to cause them harm.

In the past, and even today in some parts of the world, women have been regarded as property, beasts of burden, or worse, as slaves. They've been caricatured as weak, overly emotional, or unintelligent. Beaten down, ignored, and oppressed, women are vulnerable to the same tactics the Enemy has used for centuries. And when the devil can't get someone else to oppress the woman, he downloads lies that destroy her from within. This also disarms her ability to nurture others. When a woman believes the Enemy's lies, not only are those around her at risk, but she will eventually harm her own soul.

You'd think we would have learned by now that sometimes we are our own worst enemies. For example, the torturous custom of foot binding, which plagued China's women for over a thousand years, was perpetuated by women. Originally a symbol of female wealth and refinement, foot binding eventually became a symbol of beauty. The smaller the foot—with a three-inch foot being the ideal—the better chance the woman had of getting married.

To fit into the tiny lotus shoes, women had to literally suffer the breaking of bones in their feet, beginning when they were toddlers. They kept their feet bound for life. Though now illegal, foot binding survived for a thousand years because of women's emotional investment in the practice.[2]

Or think back to the corsets worn by women in the 1800s in Europe and America. Women in the Victorian era prized unnaturally tiny waists, and they subjected themselves and their daughters to the painfully binding contraptions, which had to be tightly laced at the back. Over time, their ribs were displaced and their lungs and other organs were compressed against the spine or shoved down into the lower abdomen. This made it hard to breathe, so ladies sometimes fainted. Thus the "feminine swoon" also became popular.

Here's what one newspaper columnist wrote about wearing a corset: "It is difficult to imagine a slavery more senseless, cruel or far-reaching in its injurious consequences than that imposed by fashion on civilized womanhood during the last generation…the tight lacing required by the wasp waist has produced generations of invalids."[3]

But we're not exempt. Today's women are tormented by the harshly thin, female-driven supermodel body image. Eating disorders are sky-rocketing. Young girls in America are now dieting as early as age ten.

Perhaps you've heard of the "thigh gap." If not, ask your teenage daughter, because she probably has. ABC News did a report on the alarming trend among high-school-aged girls, perpetuated by Internet images.[4] Standing up straight with feet together and knees touching, teens (and women) want to see gaps between their thighs even if they know it takes poor nutrition habits and over-exercising to get there.

When asked the reason for thigh gaps, a panel of young women admitted it was a status symbol—further proof that skinny frames are their ideal measure of beauty. Oddly, it is women—not their boyfriends or husbands—who pressure each other to strive for dangerously thin bodies.

Anorexia and bulimia, once confined to mostly young women, are now showing up in two other groups: young girls and older women. Anorexia has reached epidemic proportions among middle-aged women. Eating disorders now have the highest fatality rate of any mental illness.[5] Women are literally starving themselves to death to become thin.

The Female Superhero—Not So Liberating

I readily admit I love superhero movies. Remember, I was the seven-year-old wearing PF Flyers and packing my toy Winchester rifle while carrying my Baby Kitten doll.

Today's superhero movies have given us quite a rush of female superheroines splashed across our screens—a far cry from the helpless damsel in distress of years past. Perhaps these fit, strong females will provide us with better role models and higher self- esteem?

Better think again. Just when we suspected our hard-hitting heroines were saving us from our outdated images of women, this new breed of female superhero might be making things worse. A recent study shows that instead of giving women healthier views about themselves—and especially about their body images—the new superheroines may be doing just the opposite. Researchers are concerned about the impact of powerful females who have perfect bodies and perform impossible tasks (defeating bad guys and saving the world—all while wearing sexy costumes and spiked heels).

Instead of feeling empowered, women who watched these superhero images reported a dramatic drop in self-esteem and dissatisfaction with their own body images and physical appearances.[6] Thus, while the roles for women have evolved from the helpless victim to mighty protector, these superheroines may be undermining rather than improving women's perceptions of themselves and their bodies.[7]

There seems to be no end to the pressure upon women today to be perfect, much of it self-imposed. Social media has only fueled this flame. Women now have the added challenge of keeping up with the unrealistic digital world of their Facebook friends. No wonder the major emotion people report while on social media is envy.

Perhaps that's why the drug Adderall, designed to treat children with ADHD, has been hijacked for use by adult women—mostly mothers. Adderall use by women has risen a startling 750 percent in the last decade.[8] Shocked by this news? A growing number of suburban moms are becoming hooked on Adderall. They are lying to doctors and using their children's prescriptions.

Overwhelmed by their workload—trying to balance work, parenting, and household—these mothers are turning to the amphetamine to give them energy to keep pace with the frantic nature of their lives.[9] Adderall appeals to women who want to measure up to an impossible image. It allows them to work day and night, while often losing weight. One mom said she used the drug to stay up until 3:00 a.m. to clean her house. Serious side effects, such as heart attacks, strokes, and even death, don't seem to deter women from the abuse of this drug. It all sounds like the perfect storm.

There seems to be no end to the way our culture, aided and abetted by women themselves, continues to wreak havoc on females. Perhaps we don't wear corsets or bind our feet anymore. But is it any kinder for women to starve themselves to fit into size 0 jeans? What about the hyper-exercise routine required to achieve the gaunt and gnarly body most men tell me they don't even find attractive? Not to mention that an extreme loss of body fat in younger women can impede fertility. In middle-aged women, it can put them at greater risk of broken bones. Plus, life expectancy goes down when women overexercise. And I remind you that eating disorders are a number one killer. Now throw in extra-long workdays and sleep deprivation. Seriously?

The Real War on Women

Dear friend, I wonder why we keep buying the same old lies? If someone else treated a woman as badly as she sometimes treats herself—starvation, overwork, addiction, lack of rest—they'd be convicted of abuse. The real war on women may require that we take an honest look in the mirror. And to learn how to stand up to the devil, who planted those lies in the first place.

If we truly want to understand what it means to be a woman of valor, if we want to lead with kindness and teach others how to be kind, perhaps we should begin by learning how to be kind to ourselves.

> If we want to teach others how to be kind, perhaps we should begin by learning how to be kind to ourselves.

It's been said that a woman never knows how much work she can do until she sees how much has to be done. This may be true. But it would appear that many women today lack the internal boundaries to see how much work is too much until it's too late.

But I wonder if the problems run deeper than just exhaustion. Deeper than image, or people pleasing, or the desire to measure up, or to be thin, or beautiful, or rich…fill in the blank. I believe women, at their very core, are wrestling with a spiritual problem. Which takes us right back to the most important task we have on earth—one foundational to becoming a woman of valor: training our hearts to hear God's voice.

Let's not lose sight of the fact that it was her "fear of the Lord" that was central to the character of our Proverbs 31 woman of valor. Her deep faith in the Lord energized her life. That's why our foundation must be built on the solid rock of our relationship with Jesus Christ.

Finding Rest for Your Soul

This chapter is primarily about kindness. A woman of valor is kind, and she teaches others to be kind. But we're also talking here about the kindness of God. Because until we get that one right, we'll never walk in true freedom. Throughout history, we have seen how women (and all people, for that matter) have done terrible things to themselves and to each other when their view of God is off.

Once again, we have a good role model in the woman of valor in Proverbs 31. Her wholehearted devotion to God did not come from terror, but rather from a reverential awe that filled her with confidence. Such strong faith was the reason she could face her future with hope—and why she could "laugh at the days to come" (verse 25).

She knew God intimately. She had experienced Him as loving, merciful, and kind, and so she was able to lead and teach others with this same kindness. "She opens her mouth with wisdom, and the teaching of kindness is on her tongue" (verse 26 esv).

The Hebrew word *chesed*, translated *kindness* in this verse, is used throughout the Old Testament to describe God. *Chesed*, often translated *loving-kindness*, includes other aspects of God's character, such as His love and mercy. There's hardly an English equivalent that captures all that is wrapped up in *chesed*.

Scholars agree that *chesed* is one of the most important words in the entire Old Testament. Not only is it central to God's character, but it's also tied to His covenant with His people. As one scholar put it, "The covenant may be thought of as the relationship through which *chesed* flows."[10]

A covenant is sort of like a contract, only more relational and more binding. God's covenant was His way of guaranteeing His undying love and His unbreakable promises. In short, the covenant was proof of God's loving-kindness. "'With everlasting kindness [*chesed*] I will have compassion on you,' says the LORD your Redeemer" (Isaiah 54:8). The Lord is good and "his love [*chesed*] endures forever" (Psalm 107:1).

Christians believe that when Jesus came to earth, His death and resurrection marked the beginning of a new kind of covenant. Through the shedding of His blood, God provided forgiveness of our sins and a free gift of grace for all who would accept it. If this method of salvation sounds too easy, think of all it cost God.

What good news it is that Jesus now gives this invitation of salvation by grace to exhausted women—and all weary souls everywhere: "Come to me, all you who are weary and burdened, and I will give you rest. Take my yoke upon you and learn from me, for I am gentle and humble in heart, and you will find rest for your souls" (Matthew 11:28-29).

Loving-kindness, like valor, seems to be a lost art in our culture. And sadly, it's missing from many of the discussions about what it means to be a woman today. *Chesed* adds to a woman's strength instead of making her weak, as some would have us believe.

We must not forget that *chesed* is how God treats us as women.

Even when the culture is cruel, or the devil is on his rampage, or when women treat themselves and each other poorly, God covers us with His *chesed*.

Religion in particular has not been kind to women. But as I've pointed out, women also seem bent on exhausting themselves—sometimes into addictions and affairs. Today's woman seems restless. I think St. Augustine could easily have been talking to us when he made this famous statement in his *Confessions*: "You have made us for yourself, O Lord, and our heart is restless until it rests in you."[11]

A Woman's Kindest Friend

Jesus is kind to women. Just ask my friend Anya. Raised as a member of the "Untouchable" caste in India, Anya knows what it means to be treated as "less than." For centuries in India's cruel caste system, Untouchables have been regarded as less than human. People of higher castes cross the street to avoid walking on the sidewalk with Untouchables, not even wanting to be touched by their shadow.

> The life-changing message of Jesus liberates hearts.

But Anya heard the gospel of Jesus Christ as a child. She realized that only Jesus could pay the penalty for her sins—not endless sacrifices to the more than 300 million gods in Hinduism. She believed the good news that all people were created equal—to be known and loved by God.

Anya went on to attend college and graduate school, finally earning her PhD. She is married, has a family of her own, and now works with Mission India, an organization that gives hope to other women caught in poverty and oppression.[12] The life-changing message of Jesus liberates their hearts. Then education opens the door to worthwhile work and reasonable wages—transforming entire families and villages throughout India.

Jesus set Anya free, just as He has been doing for His daughters for centuries. It's the same story wherever you go. Christian missionaries ignited the movement that dismantled the gruesome custom of foot binding in China. Today, followers of Jesus are leading the efforts in the worldwide fight against the trafficking of women.

I got to see firsthand how Jesus transforms the lives of women in a remote village in southern Ethiopia. Our missionary friends had shared the gospel with this group of people a decade earlier. When the villagers first accepted Jesus, our friends immediately noticed two things: Men stopped beating their wives, and women planted flowers outside their huts. The women also became more tender mothers to their children. Better education, hygiene, and health care soon followed.

> Wherever Jesus is preached, the status of women goes up.

Wherever Jesus is preached, the status of women goes up. It was Jesus who brought true freedom in a culture that regarded women as inferior. He entrusted the message of His resurrection to a woman, appearing first to Mary Magdalene "from whom he had driven out seven demons" (Mark 16:9 GNT).

Religion has not been easy on women. But Jesus has been supremely kind. That's why I keep pointing out our enemy, the devil, as the real perpetrator of the war on women. Hurting women has been his game plan from the start.

Jesus is the only one who has ever defeated the devil. But remember, it was not a close fight. Jesus made a spectacle out of our foe and all his minions (Colossians 2:15). That's why I keep saying that abiding in Christ—drawing our strength from Him—must be our passion. Through Him, we can stand firm as women of valor, balancing the nurturer and warrior roles that make us strong and kind. God longs to meet the deepest needs of our hearts. His grace is sufficient—if only we'll regularly spend time in His presence.

It's also vitally important that we understand God's true character.

That He is our all-powerful warrior, protector, and defender. That He is infinitely kind, *chesed.* Teaching others about God's kindness begins with teaching ourselves.

Think about whether you're kind to yourself. Is it hard for you to receive God's love? Be honest. Are you exhausted? If so, Jesus wants you to find your rest in Him. And to find practical ways to rest your mind, your soul, and your body. This may mean spending more quiet time with Him or reclaiming your Sabbath and being intentional about your weekly day off. And sometimes it may be as simple as learning how to take a really good nap.

Being Kind to Yourself (Or How to Take the Perfect Nap)

A friend who was a hard worker and very productive once took the time to detail for me how she learned to take a really good nap. Over the years, she has fine-tuned her art of nap-taking. I called her the connoisseur of the perfect nap. Whenever I talk about my friend's nap method, people always seem eager for details.

Here's what she told me: First, set your alarm for one hour. Your shoes *and* socks must be off. Then you need to get all the way under your sheets—yes, even if you made your bed perfectly that morning. Finally, get a good book. Start reading, and then let yourself fall asleep naturally. The alarm will wake you, so you don't have to worry about oversleeping. Voila! There you have it. The perfect nap!

> Kindness makes people happier.

Taking a nap might seem trivial. But staying well rested is not. I hope you see by now that adequate rest is a necessity, not a luxury. God did not create us to be machines, built to work seven days a week. *Without rest, our mental and physical health will suffer. Without rest, our relationships suffer.* And sometimes even our ability to love can grow cold.

Teaching Kindness

Kindness makes people happier. Such were the findings of a recent Stanford University study. Subjects who took five kind actions each week were happier than those who did not. And those who performed more than five acts of kindness *a day* were the happiest of all. The study found that happiness is greater when the acts of kindness are directed toward those we know as opposed to strangers.[13] I guess you could say kindness, like charity, begins at home.

We've seen how our Proverbs 31 woman instructed others. I like the way the International Children's Bible puts it: "She teaches others to be kind." I would like to think her teaching about kindness started at home by teaching her own children to be kind.

Bully-Proofing Our Kids

I believe kindness is the solution to bullying and most other aggressive behaviors. Children, and even adults, may not see clearly the dangers of bullying. Some don't even understand its definition. With our own children, it helped to explain bullying to them.

Let me be clear. I think we should protect all children of all ages from bullying. Bullies don't fight fair. In my mind, two against one is always bullying. Older against younger is bullying—especially if that older one is an adult. Yes, though it's rare, an adult can sometimes bully a child. If a more powerful person is picking on a weaker one, it's bullying.

I wanted our children to learn how to fight their own battles—especially when evenly matched. But I encouraged them to tell us if they were bullied. And if I ever caught them bullying someone else—well, let's just say they caught the wrath of Mom!

The Bible tells us to defend the weak, so we can teach kindness to our children by exploring ways they can come to the aid of someone younger, weaker, or outnumbered who is being bullied. I point you back to the example of the schoolchildren in chapter 5 who discovered that by forming their "swarm" around the one being bullied, they could get the bully to leave.

Teaching our kids about kindness helps bully-proof them. We want to stop them from bullying or being bullied. And by encouraging them to stand up for those who can't stand up for themselves, we are also creating a kinder culture.

The Power of Good Nurturing

I think back to the days of nursing our three children, and I'm still awed that I was able to provide practically all the nourishment needed by those babies for their first year of life. To me, breastfeeding was nurturing and nourishment all rolled up into one.

Another reason I have enjoyed traveling in what some call "developing" nations is that I feel a kindred spirit with the common-sense mamas who live in these countries. They nurse their babies, carry them in a sling while they work, and view children as their greatest source of wealth. In all my years of traveling to Africa and teaching Bible classes to moms (who often have babies and small children at their side), I can't recall ever hearing a baby cry.

> To nurture someone is to help them grow, develop, or succeed.

To nurture someone is another way to be kind. Especially when it comes to little children. As a reminder, the words *nurture* and *nourish* come from the Latin word meaning "to nurse." To nurture someone is to help them grow, develop, or succeed. This could include providing food, protection, a place to live, or education.

Over the years, I've met all kinds of women who care for their families in all types of households all over the world. But the word *nurture* most comes alive for me when I think back to a little tent home in a slum in India—and the unlikely woman of valor who nurtured her family inside.

The Ragpicker's Wife

Men, women, and children of all ages squeezed into the patchwork tent that was both home and church for Pastor Raju. David and I were traveling through this remote slum village in India to see the work of church planters like Raju.

Raju was a ragpicker by trade. Daily, he sifted through the nearby garbage dump to find rags, plastic, bits of this-and-that to sell. It looked as if Raju had used some of "this-and-that" to construct his tent, which, though humble, was very clean and well organized inside.

Raju was also a Dalit, a member of the Untouchable caste, as were most of his neighbors. Courageous pastors like Raju were why the gospel was spreading rapidly in this region hostile to Christians.

Raju was small and wiry with a firm grip and a wide grin. He was fiery and passionate that morning as he reminded his people they were the "head and not the tail" in God's eyes. No longer did they have to be terrified of displeasing the cruel gods or being rejected by higher castes. Now their identity was secure as dearly loved children of their heavenly Father, adopted into Christ's church.

Warmth and singing filled the tent. Traditional orange marigold leis had been draped over our shoulders. Plastic chairs had been brought in for the "honored guests." David was to preach the message to Raju's church of about 50 congregants.

Raju had endured persecution. But the gaunt little warrior deeply loved his people and continued to preach the gospel. Once he went on a hunger strike until village authorities finally brought electricity into his slum neighborhood. I noticed the haphazard electrical rigging outside his tent.

But it was Raju's wife who captured my heart. Somehow she had worked her magic and turned the patchwork tent into an inviting home. Her kitchen was just a shelf, a few staples, and a one-burner hot plate in a corner of the room that was also bedroom, living room, and church.

After the service, she prepared tea along with a single roll of Ritz crackers, served to us by their children. Raju beamed as he introduced his family. A handful of boys and girls, from around 8 to 16 years of age, greeted us with shining faces and firm handshakes. They had been well nurtured there in that little one-room tent beside the garbage dump. How was this possible?

I noticed Raju's wife, though lovely in her colorful sari, looked thin and worn. (I was told that Indian mothers and fathers sometimes go without food to make sure their children have enough to eat.) But this tiny woman of valor had found a way to nurture these smiling children who were adored by their dad. She and her husband had given them physical, emotional, and spiritual nourishment. Looking into their faces, I sensed they would somehow find their way in this harsh and difficult environment.

Raju's wife was both nurturer and warrior for her little family. She's living proof that a woman of valor can live in a tent as well as a palace. Her children were a testimony that it doesn't take money or education to nurture a child—just love. And self-sacrifice. This was the legacy of the ragpicker's wife. This was her kingdom. And her husband and children were her crown.

Deborah: A Leader with Heart

I'm one of those people who gets misty-eyed over our men and women in uniform. I guess I come by this naturally. As I mentioned, my dad is a World War II submarine veteran. Our family tree is dotted with soldiers back to the Revolutionary War, when our ancestor, Captain Simon Hunt, was one of the 80 minutemen who led the charge against the British with the "shot heard round the world."

Soldiers fight for our freedom. They display courage and discipline. But for me, war is all about heart. A woman of valor is ready to fight the fight of faith and to fight for those she loves because she has heart. Remember, it's love that makes her brave.

The word *heart* is used in the Bible over 700 times. The heart is viewed as the seat of the will, the emotions, and even the entire personality. *Heart* can go hand in hand with *kindness*—as we see in the word *kindhearted*.

The heart is also connected to courage. A woman of valor has courage in the face of danger. In the Bible, the words *heart* and *courage* are sometimes used interchangeably. For example, Jesus said, "I have told you these things, so that

> A woman of valor has courage in the face of danger.

in me you may have peace. In this world you will have trouble. But take heart! I have overcome the world" (John 16:33). Instead of "take heart," several translations tell us to "take courage."

Deborah was a great leader who had heart. An Old Testament judge and prophet, she was part nurturer and part warrior. Deborah leaves us with a wonderful picture of what it means to lead with kindness.

Widely honored for her wisdom, Deborah was the first judge to be called a prophet. She spoke God's words to His people. She called them to obedience, convicted them of sin, and pointed them to God. We can be certain that Deborah had trained her heart to hear the voice of God.

In Deborah's day, Israel was in great trouble. They had strayed from the Lord and followed idols, so He sold the people into the hands of their enemies. For 20 years they had been cruelly oppressed by the Canaanites and their "900 iron chariots." As a result, they had fallen into great despair. Even their roads were unsafe, so people left their villages and retreated to the walled cities, where they hid in fear. No army of fighting warriors existed to protect Israel.

That is, until Deborah stepped on the scene. She told how "villagers in Israel would not fight…until I, Deborah, arose, until I arose, a mother in Israel" (Judges 5:7). Notice Deborah didn't refer to herself as a prophet or a judge, but as "a mother in Israel." A mother with a heart for her people. A mother ready to spring into action.

First, she commanded Barak to lead the people to war, speaking forth God's promise that He would give the enemy "into your hands" (Judges 4:6-7). Barak agreed to go only if Deborah went with him, which she did.

She correctly foretold of Israel's glorious victory against the evil Canaanite king. Afterward, she praised God in song and commended the warriors by name for their bravery. "My heart goes out to the commanders of Israel," she said to those who risked their lives (Judges 5:9 ESV). She then warned her people about the consequences of idolatry: "When new gods were chosen, then war was in the gates" (verse 8 ESV). She applauded the brave tribes who had fought and rebuked those who had refused to help. All of this was wrapped up in a glorious song of worship to God.

Deborah was a nurturing leader. And she sounds like a good mother to me. In the end, after Israel's overwhelming victory, the final line of her story tells us "the land had peace forty years" (Judges 5:31).

I wonder if God is calling forth today's women of valor to lead with strength and kindness. Women who nurture and nourish their own children. Who rise up and see potential in broken-down communities. Who look beyond someone's sin and idolatry to who she can become. Who call warriors to courage. Who give visions of victory. Who spell out sin and call for repentance. Women like Deborah, who "mother" others to greatness.

Is God calling you to be one of those women?

8

She Gives Her Life Away

She opens her hand to the poor, yes, she reaches out her filled
hands to the needy [whether in body, mind, or spirit].

PROVERBS 31:20 AMPC

t was easy to get swept up into the feminist hype of the 1970s. Promises loomed large. "You've come a long way, baby," crooned the television commercials. "You can have it all." New adventures awaited those of us willing to take the risk. I was not so much a hard-core feminist as I was an opportunist—and I was excited about the possibilities that awaited me as a woman.

Forty years later, it would seem that all should be well in the world of women. After all, we've made major strides forward in just about every area of life—business, medicine, politics…We're outpacing our male counterparts in education, earning about 60 percent of bachelor's and master's degrees and more than half of all doctorates.[1]

Women in sports have also seen dramatic progress. In the 2016 Summer Olympics in Rio, 45 percent of the athletes were women—more than double the figure from 1976. Sculpted muscles, fit bodies, power-lifting, and fast racing are no longer the sole domain of men.

And let's not forget those female superheroes flashing across our screen, leaving a trail of conquered villains—mostly male—in their wake. Girl power is used to advertise everything from sports drinks and running shoes to cosmetics and hairspray. The strong woman is here to stay. Surely today's woman is much happier than she was 40 years ago, right?

Better look again. Some troubling statistics say otherwise. Today's women report being *less* satisfied with their lives than their female counterparts in the 1970s. In *Find Your Strongest Life*, former Gallup researcher Marcus Buckingham points to data from a number of significant studies that researched a total of 1.3 million men and women surveyed over a span of several decades.

In short, women report being less happy than they were 40 years ago, and less happy than men.[2] They're also less satisfied as they age than the women of four decades ago. On top of all that, women now consume twice as much antidepression and antianxiety medication as men. Pharmaceutical companies know this full well and target these drugs aggressively—aiming about two-thirds of their commercials at women.[3]

Something is wrong in the world of women. And no one is quite sure why. Some would argue that liberation has not gone far enough—women need still more opportunities and open doors before they can be truly happy. Others are convinced we've ventured too far out of our traditional roles and believe the only answer is to turn back the clock and go home.

I wonder if the reason many of today's women are not as happy as the women of 40 years ago has something to do with the empty promises of success. Mere ambition has never been enough to satisfy any soul.

> We were created to live larger lives.

Or maybe it's because we were created to live larger lives. We've seen how God has put into us a longing to make a difference in the world. To build strong faith and strong families. To give our lives away to those who are hurting and broken.

I'll say it again: We find life as we give our lives away. It's not surprising that some of the most joyful women I know are also the most giving. Generosity and joy seem to go hand in hand. My friends Michele and Celeste started a successful jewelry-making operation called Fashion and Compassion.[4] Their nonprofit ministry has brought empowerment to hundreds of women in our city and around the world caught in the vicious cycle of poverty and human trafficking. Michele and Celeste's joy in giving life to others is contagious and has inspired others to give.

As we keep reminding ourselves, a woman of valor is part nurturer and part warrior. God has given us courage and strength to live out His purposes. What that purpose looks like will be different for each of us.

Let's remember how our woman of valor was publicly praised by her husband and children as a woman who was most blessed: "Her children rise up and call her blessed (happy, prosperous, to be admired); her husband also, and he praises her" (Proverbs 31:28 AMP).

Blessed also means "happy." The ones who knew her best spoke of her as *happy*. As she grew older, she became even happier. Instead of dreading old age, she laughed when she contemplated her future (verse 25). The woman of valor seems like a far cry from today's less-than-satisfied woman.

We Were Made for More

Somewhere along the way, I decided I wanted to save the world. Once, when I was seven, I gathered up all my allowance, tied it inside a white handkerchief, and asked my dad to give my money to some "poor children" as he traveled on a business trip through the coal-mining district of West Virginia. Dad, the former WWII sub veteran, had some "save the world" in him too. He seemed to enjoy telling me how he had discreetly dropped my stash directly in the path of some mountain children walking down the road. He drove forward far enough to avoid being noticed, but still able to watch in his rearview mirror as they discovered their treasure.

Another incident happened when I was ten. One morning I was at our neighborhood pool waiting for swim-team practice to begin. I noticed a child in the deep end. The pool wasn't yet open, so no lifeguard was on duty. The child began to flail around in the water. I realized he was drowning. *Where are all the grown-ups when you need them?* I did a fast racing dive into the pool, and with a few strong strokes I reached the deep end and pulled the child to safety. All the while wondering, *How can I be doing this?* And then, *Cool, I just saved a kid!*

I never thought much about these incidents until I was sitting in a graduate school class. We were instructed to search our memory for life-defining moments. I found myself wondering why, all these years later, I still had vivid memories of gathering up all my money to give to poor children. Or why I happened to be the only one at the pool who was available to save a drowning child that day.

Maybe you have similar stories. I wonder if you have also helped others in distress. How did that make you feel? Was there a sense of joy that you got to be the one to give aid, or help a person to safety, or perhaps save a life?

We've seen how our Proverbs 31 woman was courageous and kind. As we continue to learn more about her character, we find she was filled with compassion for the broken and had a generous spirit toward the poor: "She opens her arms to the poor and extends her hands to the needy" (Proverbs 31:20). No doubt the woman of valor had discovered the special kind of joy that comes only as we give our lives away.

We often discover the courage, strength, and compassion God gave us when we step out in faith. God calls us to join Him in His work. But even the motivation to give our lives away is not without pitfalls. We can fall into the trap of trying to be everything to everyone. In chapter 7, we saw the dangers of exhausting ourselves.

We may want to save the world, but we can't do it alone. Jesus has already saved the world, so we are simply called to serve as part of the body of Christ—that's our team. God designed us so that giving our lives to others would be a source of joy. A delight. Not a drudgery. As someone once put it, "We can't do everything for God. But we can do something."

What's Your Gift?

As I shared with you earlier, I grew tired of all the feminist zeal. And despite vows that "I would never become a Christian and would never, ever marry a minister," I found myself a sold-out believer in Jesus and happily married to a minister.

When David and I accepted the call to our first church, we moved into a fixer-upper home. I set to work on painting and wallpapering every square inch of this home all by myself. I've admitted that home-making and house-decorating skills were foreign to me at first. But I was determined to create an inviting home.

As time went on, we found ourselves struggling with infertility. The room that should have been a nursery stayed empty, so I continued to help David build the church and served everywhere I was needed. And I mean I served *everywhere*. Youth ministry, preparing meals for the sick, entertaining groups in our home…you name it. It was hard, but after all, wasn't that what a Christian was supposed to do?

Our people were wonderful and accepting—the only person putting pressure on me was me. I wrongly thought that if the work was difficult, then this must be what it meant to die to self. Lynne Hybels, wife of well-known pastor Bill Hybels, captured the feelings when she said this about her own journey: "I died to myself and my self almost died."[5]

My personal tipping point came the night I made chili for 60—and burned it—with all 60 hungry guests waiting for their meal. Thankfully they were mostly teenagers, and I salvaged enough to feed them all. But something about that experience caused me to pause and reflect:

I was drying up a little at a time. What's more, I hadn't even seen it coming.

I had dropped my old life in the corporate world and plunged head-long into what I thought God wanted me to do. I just didn't seem to be very good at it. David was patient, but it concerned him to see me trying so hard to become someone other than the woman he married. Good thing he knew me better than I knew myself.

One day on our Friday-day-off ritual of breakfast at Waffle House, he looked at me for a minute. Then as we ate our waffles, he casually said words that turned out to be life-changing for me: "Have you ever thought about going back to school—maybe for a master's degree in counseling?" His words hit their mark. I was like, *That's it...yes, that's just what I would like to do.* Why hadn't I thought of that? It made perfect sense. I could return to an academic environment, in which I thrived. Maybe I could discover how to help others and do ministry, but in a different way (besides making chili for 60). It was as if a bur-den had fallen off my back. Suddenly I could breathe again.

While working on my master's, I spent time in low-income com-munities. My practical work and internship were mostly among the poor. I found myself in parts of our city I had never seen—and lov-ing every minute of it. I was still struggling with infertility. But, as I've mentioned, serving those hurting more than I was turned out to be its own form of self-help.

During that time, I came across some words of Scripture that described what I had been learning from practical experience: "Each of you should use whatever gift you have received to serve others, as faithful stewards of God's grace in its various forms" (1 Peter 4:10).

> Use whatever gift you have received to serve others.

Various forms. I had discovered the hard way that God's grace has "various forms." And different gifts are given to us so we can be min-isters of those different forms of grace. The Greek word *charisma*, translated as "gift," is related to the word for "joy." The gifts given to us by the Holy Spirit for the purpose of building up the body of Christ are to be a source of delight. When we're using our gifts, the work we do may be hard. But our hearts should sing because we are doing what we were made to do.

This all may sound elementary to you. But remember, I was pretty new as a Christian at the time. It made good sense that God had created each individual in His church for different purposes, and that He gave us a variety of gifts so we could function as a team.

This, of course, is a book about becoming a woman of valor—not about spiritual gifts. But judging by the number of women I've seen lately who are exhausting themselves, I think a short refresher on spiritual gifts is timely for any woman who wants to give her life away.

I wonder if we're in danger of forgetting that God created each of us to be one part of the body of Christ—not a solo player. His design is that we work together so we don't exhaust ourselves. And I'll say it again: *We are stronger against the Enemy when we work together as an army.*

Where's Your Calling?

What God calls you to do may look different from the work He gives to me. The Bible seems to indicate that we are more comfortable in one of two general areas: speaking or serving.

After Peter encourages us to use the different gifts God has given to us, he follows with this word of instruction: "Do you have the gift of speaking? Then speak as though God himself were speaking through you. Do you have the gift of helping others? Do it with all the strength and energy that God supplies. Then everything you do will bring glory to God through Jesus Christ" (1 Peter 4:11 NLT).

Maybe you're high energy and practical. You see what needs to be done and get right to it. No one has to tell you to stay on task. You'll complete the job until it's done to your high standards, whether it's remodeling your home, helping to build a Habitat for Humanity house, or participating in a service project in Africa. Like the Proverbs 31 woman of valor, you "stretch out your hands to the needy," and you're motivated to relieve suffering. You're concerned about emotional distress as well as physical. Your gifts would probably lie in the areas that involve helping others, such as serving, mercy, or giving. You are encouraged to serve "with all the strength and energy that God supplies" (1 Peter 4:11 NLT).

Or perhaps you're willing to be a mouthpiece and teach truth from God's Word. You speak up for those who can't speak for themselves. Like the Proverbs 31 woman, the teaching of kindness is on your tongue, and you instruct others with wisdom. Your spiritual gifts may lie in the realm of encouragement, leadership, or teaching. Maybe you're called to write, or teach, or lead a small group.

Obviously, we all have to do both some speaking and serving as needs arise because the work simply has to get done. But we can major in the areas where we are gifted and minor in those areas where we have less interest or ability.

When we understand our spiritual gifts and combine that with what we're learning about the woman of valor, we should be able to more clearly discern God's calling on our lives.

You'll remember we saw this principle in chapter 6 when we learned how God has wired each of our children differently. And, of course, Granddaddy Chadwick's rule holds true that where our gifts and the needs we see around us intersect, we're likely to get clues about our calling.

> Experiment until you find what makes your heart sing.

What do you love to do? I encourage you to experiment until you find what makes your heart sing. It's the same as raising children. You'll serve more joyfully and last longer if you "go with your grain."

Looking back, it was graduate school that opened the door to work with various ministries of compassion. I also enjoyed teaching Bible studies. And I learned that I had extra energy for the more practical tasks, such as keeping our home in order. A woman of valor is created by God to give her life away. But the service to which He calls her, though it will often require hard work, will seem lighter because it's in keeping with her gifts.

Jesus called to His followers: "Come to me, all you who are weary and burdened, and I will give you rest…For my yoke is easy and my burden is light" (Matthew 11:28,30).

Let's remember His yoke is "easy" and the burden is "light." I especially like this modern paraphrase of these verses: "Are you tired? Worn out? Burned out on religion? Come to me. Get away with me and you'll recover your life. I'll show you how to take a real rest. Walk with me and work with me—watch how I do it. Learn the unforced rhythms of grace. I won't lay anything heavy or ill-fitting on you. Keep company with me and you'll learn to live freely and lightly" (Matthew 11:28-30 MSG).

Courage to Say Yes to God

God's task for you may be a good fit—but sometimes saying yes to His call can be scary. A woman may never know how much courage she has until she steps out in faith to go where God sends her.

This happened when my friend Barb, along with her husband, Don, sensed God calling them to the mission field in Africa. With four-year-old Mark and two-year-old Nancy, they set out for Ethiopia. Accepting this calling to Africa meant saying good-bye to family and friends, as well as to ministry in Bryan, Ohio, and the church they'd grown to love. And this was in the 1960s, a time without the communication technology we enjoy today.

Barb was just 24 when she was deeply moved by a presentation made by some missionaries from Ethiopia in the church Don pastored. But she was terrified at the thoughts going through her mind. She told the Lord, "Anywhere but Africa!" She had never even been on an airplane. And the thought of snakes terrified her.

But she felt God calling them to go. Although they hadn't discussed it, Don felt the same pull. Barb says when he asked for anyone who felt called to Ethiopia to come to the front of their small church, "I could hardly believe that my feet carried me right up front and my pounding heart was completely willing—even if it meant trading everything we loved—for Africa!"

Barb and Don packed up their children and left the comforts of home to take the gospel into remote areas in Ethiopia. They saw God at work in tough places— but also experienced the great joy of giving their lives in service.

After a period of intense training in Ethiopia, they left for their first assignment. Barb was shocked upon arrival to learn that to get to their village, their family would have to travel up the side of a steep mountain, elevation 9000 feet!

The path up the mountain was narrow, and there were no guardrails. The only mode of transportation? On the back of a mule. Mark was almost six, Nancy was four, and now they had five-month-old Dan. Plus, it was Barb's first time on anything with four legs, so you can just imagine the exciting and frightening journey up that mountain. It took five hours!

Barb and Don tell this and other stories in a book of memories they wrote about their adventures in Ethiopia.[6]

I read their book before Barb and I met. I could tell she was a loving and devoted mother. But answering God's call to go to Ethiopia involved some risk to her family. Just reading the accounts of how God kept them safe and protected their children throughout their time in Africa expanded my own view of God.

I remember thinking that the problems I was facing in my own life seemed small in comparison to what Barb had to deal with. *If God can help Barb ride on a mule's back up the side of a mountain for five hours with three little children, He can surely take care of my situation.* Barb raised my bar of faith, helping me learn to trust God more in hard places.

When I met Barb, she and Don had become members of our church. Their five children were all grown, and they had ten grandchildren. Barb was also waging a courageous fight with cancer. Sadly, our friendship was measured in months rather than years, for she lost her battle with cancer a short time after we met.

But I view Barb as a true woman of valor. She had trained her heart to hear God's voice. She understood what it meant to give her life to the broken and hurting. Her rock-solid relationship with Jesus had made an impact on her husband and children. Her infectious joy, strong courage, and sense of humor had blessed others. Even during her illness, she bore witness to God's great strength working through her.

Three months before Barb died, we held a women's gathering at our church. As part of my message, I shared some of Barb's stories (especially the one about the mule ride up that mountain). I planned to have an opportunity for Barb to sell and sign her book. But I was a little concerned because I knew she had been growing weaker.

Yet Barb showed up that night looking amazingly strong. Hundreds of women came to the event. Many waited in line to talk to Barb and to buy her book and have her sign it. She smiled and talked with each one. The books sold out. Women are still talking about Barb and her stories of God's great faithfulness.

Barb remains a shining example of a woman of valor who had the courage to say yes to God. She left a legacy to her family and those around her of what God can do through a woman who hears and obeys His call.

Fighting Forward

It took 96 months of surgeries, medications, treatments, and prayer before the births of all three of our children. God taught me some of my most valuable lessons during those years of "wait training." I learned to persevere. And David and I learned to lean on each other.

> Fight forward. Serving is self-help. When you are hurting, give life to others. Draw close to God.

Even after all three of our children came, these lessons remained: Fight forward. Serving is self-help. When you are hurting, give life to others. Draw close to God.

I hovered between my dream to have children and trying to live well in the moment. Working on my master's degree led me to serve among the urban poor, and eventually that led to humanitarian work overseas.

Since that time, I've delivered relief kits to Darfur. Visited slums in India. Worked on tribal reconciliation projects and a school for genocide survivors in Rwanda. I've traveled to the Middle East to partner with groups serving the war-ravaged Syrian and Iraqi refugees. I've seen the human spirit struggle to find hope in the darkest of places.

Some say we should live to give. I discovered that I could give to live. The promise of Scripture has proven true again and again: "If you spend yourselves in behalf of the hungry and satisfy the needs of the oppressed, then

> Some say we should live to give. I discovered that I could give to live.

your light will rise in the darkness, and your night will become like the noonday" (Isaiah 58:10).

Giving my life to others has brought healing and relief to me and filled my empty places. I would say to God, "I'm entrusting my business into Your hands while I work on Your business." And I would feel His peace inside me even before the healing occurred.

And healing did come—in a rather dramatic manner. Into our fourth year of waiting, it was clear that medical science had come up short. The last in our string of doctors looked at our most recent surgical report and delivered the blow. Endometriosis had done its damage, and my fallopian tubes were scarred completely shut. Our chances of getting pregnant, even with surgery, were practically nil. David and I sat stunned, letting the news sink in.

The doctor scheduled major surgery—a last-ditch effort to laser the web of scar tissue. The night before surgery, something happened that even our doctor couldn't explain.

I was channel surfing on our television, trying to keep my mind off the surgery I faced the next day, when I was drawn to a program where the Christian minister on the screen was praying for various needs, including healing. The man paused, and then said quietly, "Someone watching this program has scar tissue. It could be in their lungs... no, it's in her abdomen. I sense I'm to tell you that God is healing you right now."

"Scar tissue." Was this real? I wanted to believe this could be for me. Scar tissue was the mountain I faced and the exact words of the doctor's diagnosis. Being a note taker, I wrote down the words spoken by the minister and the exact time and date.

The next morning in surgery, our doctor found something quite unexpected. My tubes—which had been so severely scarred—were perfect! The doctor closed me up after a few minutes instead of the expected four hours of surgery. "Your tubes are perfect," he told me later, perplexed. "There's no sign of a problem; absolutely no scar tissue anywhere."

Six weeks after that surgery and exactly 48 months from the start of my infertility journey, we conceived our Bethany. Three years later, we had DB. And just before I turned 40, I delivered Michael.

My life, once in part defined by infertility and medical procedures, became filled with PTA meetings, basketball games, swim meets, proms, weddings, and now grandchildren.

> Seasons of waiting are not wasted.

God has a flair for the dramatic. He parted the seas, raised the dead, walked on water, opened blind eyes, healed paralytics. God's miracles are sometimes big and full of drama.

But through my experience of waiting for babies, I've grown to believe some of His best miracles happen slowly. This does not make them any less magnificent. Seasons of waiting are not wasted. I remain a big dreamer. I continue to fight forward. I wait with hope because I really do believe in miracles.

Ruth: From Life-Giver to World-Changer

Ruth is the only woman in the entire Bible to be singled out by name as a woman of valor. She is one of just two women to have a book of the Bible named after her. Plus, she ended up in the lineage of Jesus, one of the four women listed in the genealogy in Matthew chapter 1.

Yet there is nothing in the early life of Ruth to suggest she would end up as one of Scripture's most noble women. Her story began with a famine, and things only got worse from there.

Naomi and her husband and sons left home in Bethlehem and traveled to Moab because of the famine. Conditions there were hard. The Moabites were a heathen culture that practiced hideous idolatry and even human sacrifice. They were not nice people.

Famine itself was grinding enough. Then Naomi's husband died. What started as a temporary stay in Moab dragged on and on. Her two sons married women from Moab. But after ten long years, the sons also died. Naomi was stricken.

Certainly God was punishing her, she thought. Destitute, she prepared to travel back home with her daughters-in-law, renaming herself *Mara*, which means "bitter." But then, because neither of Naomi's daughters-in-law had children, she encouraged them to go back to their own people and their own gods and try to remarry. One did so, but Ruth refused and clung to Naomi.

When Naomi saw Ruth was determined to go with her, she stopped urging her to return to her own people. Ruth, a heathen from Moab, pledged undying devotion not only to Naomi, but to God: "Your people will be my people and your God my God…May the LORD deal with me, be it ever so severely, if even death separates you and me" (Ruth 1:16-17).

Ruth's strong stand appears to be the simple kindness and fervent devotion of a young woman to her widowed mother-in-law. But her sacrificial act, the giving of her life for Naomi, not only saved Naomi's life but brought about a destiny and a blessing for Ruth that would change the world forever.

Naomi and Ruth returned to Bethlehem. The villagers were amazed at Ruth's devotion to her mother-in-law. Even the elders spoke to one another of her loyalty. When she finally met Boaz, the man she would eventually marry, Boaz assured her that "everyone in town knows that you are a woman of valor" (Ruth 3:11 TLV).

Ruth, the outsider and a Gentile, married Boaz, the nearest "guardian-redeemer" (Ruth 3:9). This meant he could buy the land formerly owned by Naomi's deceased husband, but he would acquire Ruth as a wife with the land. Little did they know that the son to be born to them, Obed, would one day have a grandson named David, who would become King David. Ruth, Naomi, and their tiny village would also have been awestruck to learn that Ruth and her son would be listed by name in the lineage of Jesus (Matthew 1:2-16).

Perhaps we would say Ruth was honored because she was devoted to her family. Or because she was especially kind, which is also true. But I'd like to think it was her devotion to the one true God, whose life she had seen reflected all those years through Naomi. She was willing to give up the false gods of her people to serve this God.

God used an unlikely woman, a heathen, to be an instrument of redemption. And we learn, once again, about the *chesed*, or kindness of God.

When you think God has forgotten you; when you've endured grinding poverty or hunger or war; when those closest to you have died; when you feel ashamed and forsaken; when you are bitter about your losses, remember this: You are not beyond God's *chesed*. His grace will never fail. Therefore it is still possible to have hope.

And sometimes hope comes from the place you least expect it. Naomi's hope came from a Gentile woman. An outsider. God loves the outsider. The broken. The weak and sick and poor. The heathen with a heart for Him. And anyone who turns to Him in faith will be saved.

Something Beautiful for God

Mother Teresa dared to leave her comfortable life to serve the destitute in India. Her work was celebrated the world over when she was canonized as a saint in September of 2016. Some people have wondered about the revelation that she had endured an extended "dark night of the soul," and how she persevered.[7] Mother was not a depressed woman, according to close personal friend and long-time spiritual advisor, Bishop William Curlin. He said she came to look at the darkness as an opportunity to share in the sufferings of Christ. And, as she put it, "to love Jesus in the night."[8]

Curlin explained that Mother Teresa would find joy when she looked for Jesus in the faces of those she served—the hungry child or the dying leper. "My hands are the hands of Jesus," she would tell him. "My eyes are the eyes of Jesus."

"She truly believed that every morning, God wanted to say to us as believers, 'Wake up now. I want to walk the earth in *you* today.'" Always be on the lookout, she encouraged, for opportunities to "bring Christ's presence to everyone you touch."[9]

So compelling was Mother Teresa's life of service that the hard-boiled atheistic journalist, Malcolm Muggeridge, turned to Christ after extensive interviews with her. These interviews resulted in his biography of her life, *Something Beautiful for God*.

Paul encouraged women to adorn themselves with good deeds, which would make them—like Mother Teresa—beautiful. Or as The Message paraphrases it, we should be "doing something beautiful for God and becoming beautiful doing it" (1 Timothy 2:10 MSG).

A Dangerous Prayer

One of the most dangerous prayers you can pray—and one of the most powerful—is this one: "Lord, break my heart for what breaks Yours." When I have sincerely prayed that prayer, God's answers have come in unusual and often dramatic ways. At times this prayer has been answered so quickly that I've coined the term "hot prayers."

God has broken my heart many times. For the Christians who were the target of genocide in Sudan, for survivors in Rwanda and Burundi, for Syrian refugees fleeing ISIS, and for families in the fragile neighborhoods in my own community. My heart continually breaks for those in any nation or neighborhood who don't know Jesus and face a Christless eternity.

There's plenty these days to break our hearts. But God's grace abounds. More are turning to Christ in formerly closed nations than ever before. Here in America, people are grasping for hope. And whether or not they know it, many are thirsty for the gospel.

> "If God be your partner, make your plans large."

As you've reflected on your own gifts and calling, my prayer is that God will show you where He needs you most. The Proverbs 31 woman of valor lived an ordinary life largely at home with her family, but with uncommon faithfulness, love, excellence, courage, and kindness. Her life and her works brought the rewards of recognition from her family and community. Her husband and children gave her praise and honor. "Let her works bring her praise" (verse 31). "Many women do noble things, but you surpass them all" (verse 29).

The great evangelist D.L. Moody is said to have issued this powerful challenge to his sons from his deathbed: "If God be your partner, make your plans large." The woman of valor dares to go to God and say, "Use me. Send me to the broken of this world."

A Larger Life

I've done a complete 180-degree turn from my life as an agnostic in the 1970s to a pastor's wife with years of experience teaching and counseling women. I'm convinced that much of the advice for women—even so-called Christian advice—falls short of God's design for us. And after countless conversations with women of all ages and stages, I have come to this simple realization: Most women are not living large enough lives—and deep down inside, they know it. Women want their lives to count. That's because God created us to be women of valor.

Proverbs 31:30 stands as a sobering reminder to women today who are being seduced to live for the moment and worship self: "Charm is deceptive, and beauty is fleeting; but a woman who fears the LORD is to be praised."

If the researchers got it right, women are not as happy today as they were 40 years ago, and many reasons for this are suggested. But I'm not so sure the reasons are complex. The secret to a happier life is not simply more opportunities, the perfect marriage, the best kids, the most well-decorated home, the highest paying job, the best wardrobe or work-out body, or the coolest vacations. It's something far more. The secret of a happier life rests in knowing God deeply and experiencing His unconditional love— and then pouring that love out to those who are thirsty. Loving God and loving our neighbor as only a woman of valor can.

> The woman of valor is sometimes fierce, but always kind.

The woman of valor can be any one of us. She need not have money, or power, or fame. She can be married or single, with or without children, young or old, and from any nation or people group on the earth. But she dares to dream big and love deeply. It's love that makes her brave.

She defends the weak and gives generously to the poor. She builds her home and her family with wisdom. And she strengthens herself to be ready for her daily challenges. She abides in the Lord. Her spiritual roots run deep, so she's armed and ready to meet the attacks of the Enemy. The woman of valor is sometimes fierce, but always kind. She is a woman of hope. And she gives hope to others. Are you ready to say yes to God's calling for such a time as this?

9

She Is Destined to Reign

Speak up for those who cannot speak for themselves...
Speak up and judge fairly;
defend the rights of the poor and needy.

PROVERBS 31: 8-9

What is there about a princess that captures our imagination? Just ask any five-year-old. She'll likely tell you a princess is kind and brave. Plus, you get to live in a real castle and wear pretty dresses. You might have to fight against mean people. Sometimes a handsome prince will come and help you out when things get really bad. And he might just become your husband because true love is like that. Whatever happens, it's okay, because if you're a real princess, you can tell a lot of people what to do and they will have to do it. Things usually work out in the end, and you get to live happily ever after.

No matter how cynical the world becomes, the princess is here to stay. At least that's the opinion of a British writer and self-described "feminist mom." In her *New York Times* editorial about the relevance of British royalty, she asks why we even need a princess job description today "when news events are grim and no one believes in fairy tale endings and women no longer wait around to see if the glass slipper fits."[1]

But "princessing" has changed, she maintains, and is "good, hard work these days." She tells her feminist friends not to worry when their daughters want to dress up as princesses because being a princess gives girls a chance to be the heroes in their own stories. Girls gravitate to princesses the way boys do to action heroes. "Don't worry if your five-year-old girl insists on a pink frilly princess dress," she advises. "It doesn't mean she wants to subside into froth; it just means, sensibly enough for her, that she wants to take over the world."[2]

On some level, I agree with her. There is something quite heroic about being a princess. And from my experience raising a daughter and observing granddaughters, no one has to teach little girls to role-play the part of a princess—it just comes naturally.

But instead of being princesses who merely "take over the world," I'd like to think God designed us as women of valor with a more heroic mission. He has called us to give our lives away to our families, to our communities, and to the hurting and broken world around us.

> Every woman has a little bit of princess in her. And deep down inside, she believes she can change the world.

We've explored the nurturer and warrior themes woven by God into the hearts of women. He has provided plenty of role models to encourage our quest to become women of valor. Women like Esther, Ruth, and the Proverbs 31 woman are celebrated throughout the pages of Scripture.

I believe every woman has a little bit of princess in her. And deep down inside, she believes she can change the world. She desires to use her powerful influence for good and to give life to others. History points us to courageous and noble women who poured themselves out in service to others. One such woman of valor was a medieval queen in the country of Scotland.

The Real Princess Diaries

A long time ago there lived a real princess who *did* change the world. Her name was Margaret. She married a Scottish king and thus became Queen Margaret, one of the most beloved nobles in the history of Scotland.

I became captivated by her story years ago when traveling with our family through the Scottish highlands. It was easy to be mesmerized by the land of castles, kings, kilts, and battlefields.

Years later, while I was writing this book about the woman of valor, memories of Queen Margaret came flooding back to my mind. Perhaps you'll agree with me that Margaret embodies much of what we have been learning about the biblical woman of valor.

Her story takes us back to the Middle Ages. Margaret of Wessex was an English princess born in Hungary to Princess Agatha of Hungary and English Prince Edward the Exile around 1045. Her parents fled to Hungary as exiles after the Danes took over England.

When Margaret was ten years old, she and her family returned to England, where her father suddenly died before he could assume the throne. Years later, Margaret and her mother, along with her two siblings, were forced to, once again, flee for their lives when William the Conqueror stormed his way through England.

While sailing north, Margaret and her family were caught in a storm and shipwrecked on the coast of Scotland. They were aided by King Malcolm and put under his protection. Before long, Malcolm fell deeply in love with the beautiful and kind princess. Margaret and Malcolm married in 1070 at the castle in Edinburgh.

We've been learning about the strong influence a woman of valor can have on her own family. We see such an example in Margaret, a deeply committed Christian whose faith influenced the rather uncouth Malcolm. He turned his heart to God, largely because of his wife. The couple had six sons and two daughters and raised all of them to become strong followers of Christ.

So respected was Margaret for her wisdom that Malcolm placed her in charge of all Scotland's domestic affairs. She was often consulted on other state matters as well. Malcolm couldn't read or write, so Margaret often read him stories from the Bible. Her example also had an impact on the quality of Malcolm's reign, helping him become what was known as the "just ruler." Together they prayed, fed the hungry, and served the needy.

Margaret had a heart for Scotland's poor, showing special kindness to orphans. She fed the hungry every morning in the castle, even before she had her own breakfast. She was also known for her deep life of prayer, rising early for prayer and reading the Bible.

Margaret worked to strengthen the church in Scotland and helped change areas that needed reform. She also encouraged the ordinary Scottish people to live as faithful Christians, emphasizing prayer and a holy lifestyle.

Margaret helped bring a more refined culture to the somewhat barbaric Scotland of the eleventh century. She promoted the arts and education and encouraged traders from other lands to bring beautiful articles of clothing and furniture to the people. She even introduced the tartan plaids, the distinctive costume for which the Scots are known.[3]

The chroniclers all agree in depicting Queen Margaret as a strong, pure, noble character, who had very great influence over her husband, and through him over Scottish history, especially in the area of reforming the church.[4] Some called her "The Pearl of Scotland." In 1250, Pope Innocent IV canonized Margaret as a saint, acknowledging her life of holiness and extraordinary virtue.

When learning about Margaret's vast areas of service to Scotland, I couldn't help but notice the quieter but equally important impact she had on her eight children. Besides educating them, she instilled a strength of faith and character that set the foundation for three of her six sons to become Scottish kings during what was known as Scotland's

"Golden Era." As she had done with King Malcolm, she is said to have influenced her sons to become just and holy rulers.

Margaret was born into royalty—not what you would call an ordinary woman. But she shows what can happen when a woman of great influence chooses to use her position to accomplish God's purposes.

Strong in faith, kind to the poor, wise in matters of culture and trade, devoted to her family, Queen Margaret of Scotland gives us another example of a woman of valor. Her life of daily abiding in Christ and giving her life away to others influenced her husband and children, as well as those around her. Who can measure the full impact, not just on Scottish history, but on the history of Christendom, because of the life of one woman of valor?

The Training of a King

While we are exploring the world of kings and queens, let's go back and take a final look at the woman of valor in Proverbs 31. We have been studying the characteristics of the woman of valor (in verses 10-31). But if we examine the very beginning of the chapter, we find a set of instructions from the queen mother to her son who would be king. These words are the teaching of the mother of King Lemuel.

Bible scholars are divided about the identity of King Lemuel. Some think *Lemuel*, which means "devoted to God," was another name for Solomon. Others believe it was a name for King Hezekiah. Some have concluded that King Lemuel is the fictitious representation of the ideal king. Whoever it was, he had a wise mother. Her words are regarded as prophetic words of Scripture, "an inspired utterance his mother taught him" (verse 1).

The word in this verse translated as *taught* implies much more than mere verbal instruction. It can mean "to chasten, reprove, discipline, correct, or instruct."[5] This kind of training implies continual reinforcement. It doesn't happen quickly and best occurs within the context of a close relationship, such as a mother with her children.

King Lemuel's mother begins her prophecy by referring to her son as the "answer to my prayers!" (verse 2). In the following verses, she teaches him important life lessons about how to behave in a kingly manner, perhaps in much the same way that Queen Margaret taught her sons. We catch a glimpse into the heart of this mother who had prayed for her son and devoted him to the Lord. Let's look closer at the teachings that were foremost in her mind as she trained the son who would be king:

Proverbs 31:1-9

The sayings of King Lemuel—an inspired utterance his
    mother taught him:
Listen, my son! Listen, son of my womb!
    Listen, my son, the answer to my prayers!
Do not spend your strength on women,
    your vigor on those who ruin kings.
It is not for kings, Lemuel—
    it is not for kings to drink wine,
    not for rulers to crave beer,
lest they drink and forget what has been decreed,
    and deprive all the oppressed of their rights.
Let beer be for those who are perishing,
    wine for those who are in anguish!
Let them drink and forget their poverty
    and remember their misery no more.
Speak up for those who cannot speak for themselves,
    for the rights of all who are destitute.
Speak up and judge fairly;
    defend the rights of the poor and needy.

The queen mother's words are instructions about the kind of king he should be. Like any good mother, she warned him about the dangers of immoral women and overindulgence in alcohol. But her cautions appear to have had more to do with his calling as king rather than mere morality.

For example, she tells him loose women "ruin kings" and drinking can cause a king to forget laws and deprive the oppressed of their rights. She challenges her son to use his power to help the broken, "[speaking] up for those who cannot speak for themselves" and "[defending] the rights of the poor and needy" (Proverbs 31:3,5,8-9).

Clearly the queen mother saw the potential dangers of royalty even more than her son did. And much like Queen Margaret, she demonstrated her concern that he would be a just and kind ruler to the poor.

If King Lemuel's mother prayed for this son before he was born and during his lifetime, surely she also prayed for his wife. So the description of the woman of valor, which we have been exploring (verses 10-31), could easily reflect the heart's desire of a mother as she prays for her son's future wife. This, of course, makes her instructions about seeking a woman of valor all the more meaningful. And isn't this the prayer for every mother of sons?

As we continue to reflect on the character qualities of the woman of valor, I'd like to think these verses also represent a mother's specific hopes and dreams for the kind of woman of valor her daughters would one day become.

Mighty Men, Women of Valor

When we accept Jesus as our Lord, we immediately become royalty—sons and daughters of the King. We are called to be "mighty in the land" (Psalm 112:2). The Bible gives us plenty of heroes to show us how to be mighty—to live as victorious and courageous men and woman of God.

Heroes provide us with role models. But they also make our task of training a little easier. Their stories help us stay focused. They give us energy to work toward our dreams. And as my kids would tell me when they were younger, heroes make learning "way more fun." There's a rea-son film writers give us superheroes. Not super textbooks, super teachers, or super leaders.

Heroes provide us with role models.

We would agree that all epic tales have some version of the hero who dares greatly to follow a quest to overcome evil and bring good to oth-ers. The greater the obstacles the hero must face and the more costly the personal sacrifices, the more thrilling the story. And the more triumphant the victory. No wonder we love movies like *Lord of the Rings* or *Star Wars*.

The Bible is honest about the messy lives of some of its heroes. If we feel less than adequate, or if we think we're not courageous enough for God's purposes, we can draw strength from their example.

We've seen how God worked mightily through women of valor such as Esther, Ruth, and Deborah. But the Lord also gave His power to a woman named Rahab, whose valor rose out of a life of broken-ness. Rahab was a prostitute in Jericho and certainly a far cry from roy-alty. Yet she risked her life to protect the spies sent by Joshua to check out the city before battle. She hid them in her home, at great peril to her personal safety.

She acknowledged that their God was the true God. Before the spies lay down for the night, she went up on her roof and said to them:

> I know that the LORD has given you this land and that a great fear of you has fallen on us, so that all who live in this country are melting in fear because of you. We have heard how the LORD dried up the water of the Red Sea for you when you came out of Egypt, and what you did to Sihon and Og, the two kings of the Amorites east of the Jordan, whom you completely destroyed. When we heard of it, our hearts melted in fear and everyone's courage failed because of you, for the LORD your God is God in heaven above and on the earth below (Joshua 2:8-11).

Rahab's courage and kindness secured her safety and that of her entire family. What's more, she lived out the rest of her days married to an Israelite and part of their community. She even went on to become the mother of Boaz, whom you'll remember as the honorable man who married Ruth. Rahab lived the rest of her life as a transformed woman. She is one of only four women listed by name in the lineage of Jesus (Matthew 1:5).

Then there's the example of Gideon, who certainly felt less than adequate. Gideon was the youngest in his family. The people of Israel had done evil in the Lord's eyes, so He handed them over to their enemies. "Israel became very weak…and the Israelites cried out to the LORD" (Judges 6:6 CEB).

The Lord sent His angel to Gideon with this message: "The LORD is with you, O mighty man of valor" (Judges 6:12 ESV). To which Gideon replied something like, "Who me? I'm just a nobody. I'm the youngest in my family. Our clan is the weakest in the whole tribe."

"Mighty man of valor," or *gibbor chayil*, was a term used to describe warriors. Heroes. Champions. Not a guy who was the least in his family, from the lowest clan in a beaten-down nation. But God must have seen something in Gideon, because He said to him, "You have strength, so go and rescue Israel from the power of Midian. Am I not personally sending you?" The Lord added, "Because I'm with you, you'll defeat the Midianites as if they were just one person" (Judges 6:14-16 CEB).

And that's just what happened. God walked Gideon through each of his doubts and fears. Then He asked Gideon to do some hard things. Gideon's brave actions saved Israel, and he became a new man in the process—a mighty man of valor.

So you see, the Bible's heroes are not perfect role models. They are flawed men and women. God allows us to see their weaknesses so we can be sure that the real power comes from God

> God desires that we, too, become heroes in His kingdom.

Himself. That means any of us can become a woman of valor or a mighty warrior if we will yield our lives to God and trust Him for our strength. God desires that we, too, become heroes in His kingdom.

Called to Be World-Changers

If we believe in Jesus, the Bible tells us we become even more than just heroes in God's kingdom. We are now sons and daughters who are a royal priesthood—royalty in training. Royalty is no longer reserved for priests and kings, those born into royal lineage. As brothers and sisters in Christ, we are part of God's royal family. "You are a chosen people, a royal priesthood, a holy nation, God's special possession, that you may declare the praises of him who called you out of darkness into his wonderful light" (1 Peter 2:9).

God sees within each of us the courage and strength He has put there. Even if we feel broken, like Rahab. Or if our family, or clan, or nation is a mess, like Gideon's. God loves us when we're weak. But He delights in making us strong. We may feel exhausted, rejected, ignored, empty, or afraid. If so, His words to us are His words to Gideon: "Because I am with you, you will defeat your enemies."

> God loves us when we're weak. But He delights in making us strong.

What are your enemies? Job loss, depression, marriage problems, a rebellious child, infertility, loneliness? Maybe you struggle with a feeling of inadequacy and fear like Gideon did. Perhaps God is whispering to you right at this moment as He whispered to Gideon: "The Lord is with you, mighty warrior, man [or woman] of valor. And because I am with you, you will have strength to prevail!"

We are God's royal priesthood. Citizens of a kingdom not of this world—a kingdom that dwells in our hearts. As we live in that newness of life to which we are called, our good works are to bring glory to God. "Dear friends, I urge you...Live such good lives among the pagans that, though they accuse you of doing wrong, they may see your good deeds and glorify God" (1 Peter 2:11-12).

I mentioned earlier that I asked my husband, David, how he saw me as a fighter—a woman of valor. He said he saw me fighting hard for our children's dreams. But he's observed another kind of fight as well. He said he saw me fighting to defend the character of God—especially to those who don't yet know Him. It's true. I believe people cannot worship and serve God unless they understand Him to be all-good, all-loving, and all-powerful.

I believe we are called to make God's goodness shine forth as glorious and His virtues to be on display. Our good works simply point to the wonderful character of our heavenly Father and cause others to "glorify God" (1 Peter 2:12). This is how we fight. This is how we overcome evil with good. This is how we do war.

The woman of valor may be one who serves in the inner city. Or she could be the queen of Persia, like Esther. Perhaps she is a ragpicker's wife or a missionary to Africa. Maybe she is a young doctor serving the poor, or a mother in Burundi, or even a medieval Scottish queen. Or perhaps she is *you*.

> Let us become women of valor who dare to do something beautiful for God and become beautiful doing it.

Dear friend, if this stirs your soul, maybe God is calling you at this time in history to be a woman of valor. He has given you strength and courage and equipped you with a unique set of gifts. He has entrusted you with life experiences and, yes, even a few hard trials that have prepared you to understand the suffering of others.

Someplace—a household and a community somewhere—desperately needs your love. A cause has your name on it. And there is the greatest mission of all, to reach the world for Christ. God issues us this noble challenge: Let us become women of valor who dare to do something beautiful for God and become beautiful doing it.

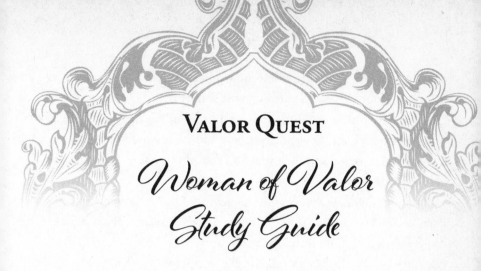

Valor Quest

Woman of Valor Study Guide

Dear Friend,

I don't know your name, or why the Lord prompted you to learn about the woman of valor. But it has been my fervent prayer that God will encourage your heart. I hope He tells you that you are loved, chosen, and specially created by Him for the purpose only you can fulfill. And that you are fearfully and wonderfully made—a nurturer and a warrior all wrapped into one. He wants to bless you so you will be a blessing to others (Genesis 12:2). When you are functioning in your "sweet spot" as a woman of valor, those around you will flourish.

I did not go looking for the woman of valor. I guess you could say she found me. If I hadn't stumbled onto the beautiful translation of *eshet chayil* in the Orthodox Jewish Bible, "woman of valor," I would never have written a book on the Proverbs 31 woman. What else could possibly be said on the subject of "biblical womanhood"?

But I got excited as I began digging into the Hebrew and Greek texts, exploring dozens of English translations, and looking back at history. God delights in revealing new insights from His holy Word. And as I reflected on the lives of ordinary women of valor I have known—well, their stories just had to be told.

God's ways are higher than our ways. There is always something new to learn. And learning about the woman of valor is perhaps the most inspiring thing I've learned in quite some time.

But I'll let you in on a little secret. I asked God, straight up, if He really was calling me to write this book. I knew it would be a lot of work, and I have a crazy, busy life. So I tossed out a fleece. Yep, just like Gideon.

I prayed, *Lord, am I hearing You correctly? Are You really asking me to write about the woman of valor?* The woman of valor concept has been somewhat ignored in Christian circles, but I found her to be widely celebrated in the Jewish world. My specific prayer went something like this: *Lord, if You truly are calling me to write about the woman of valor, please have a Messianic Jew—someone whom I have never met—cross my path.*

Over the next week or so, three different Jewish believers I had never met reached out to me. Not one but three encounters with Jews who follow Jesus! Amazing! Out of the blue, one of the women introduced herself through an email to share how she had been attending our church and had quietly accepted Christ while sitting with her husband in our worship service one morning.

So when the writing became difficult, or when my laptop had a meltdown, or when family crises hit during the daunting process, I kept going back to my sense of God's call. And to His threefold answer to my "fleece."

I believe your life will be forever changed as you learn what God's Word has to say on the subject of the woman of valor. I hope you can take the time to prayerfully complete the "Valor Quest." We live in a time when women seem thirsty for the truth. I also pray God will show you a handful of women to take on this journey with you. Dear friend, will you join me in praying that God will raise up an army of women? Women of valor who want to change their world.

Together in our quest,

Marilynn

Before You Begin

Maybe you're confused by all the voices telling you how to live as a biblical woman. The purpose of this book is not to explore one more "how to" method. Rather, I invite you on a different quest—to discover what it means to be a woman of valor.

Remember, God is creative and He never does things the same way twice. He has designed your journey especially for you. It's important to allow enough time to earnestly seek the Lord. You may find you need to rest more. Move at a slower pace.

I'll guide you through some biblical truths and share practical tips I've learned along the way. But the real fun begins when you start to discover the path God has marked out for you as a woman of valor— that's your unique story.

We'll take a deeper look at our Proverbs 31 woman, along with a few of her courageous sisters. The Bible is filled with women who changed history. As we explore their stories, let's look for clues about how to become a woman of valor in today's world. I'll also introduce you to some ordinary women like my friends Barbara in chapter 1 and Heather in chapter 5, who became extraordinary as they stepped out in faith to obey God.

Our quest will be challenging. My own journey has taken me way out of my comfort zone. But I believe you'll discover the courage and strength that God has already given you as you step out in faith to obey His voice.

God didn't design our quest to be an easy one. He knows us too well for that—most women won't seek a treasure too easily found. In fact, most of us would rather fight for a prize that demands too much of us than too little.

I believe you're ready to live large for God as a woman of valor. Someone once said that God's plans for us are far better than our own dreams. My fervent prayer is that this adventure will open doors to a richer and more fulfilling life than you ever dreamed possible!

Format

- Read each chapter in the book before you complete the questions for that chapter.

- Find a place where you feel close to God to read your Bible and pray.

- Carve out enough quiet time each day for this material to really stick.

Tools to Enrich Your Study

A Bible

Use your favorite translation or version. Or invest in the fantastic *Hebrew-Greek Key Word Study Bible*. (It's author Beth Moore's personal favorite.) You can get it in leather for less than the cost of a pair of running shoes. I've been using this version for years.[1]

A Journal

Any kind will do. I prefer the Moleskine Classic.

Chubby Book

A wire-bound booklet of 3 x 5-inch index cards. You can find Oxford Spiral Index Cards at target.com for under two dollars. (I also like to use a fine-point Sharpie.)

Online Resources

BibleGateway.com is my favorite. Simply click onto one of dozens of English translations. You can also study the Greek words by selecting the *MOUNCE Reverse-Interlinear New Testament* (MOUNCE). https://www.biblegateway.com

1

She Is a Fierce Fighter

A woman of valor can be any age or stage in her life. She may be a wife and mother. Or she may be serving God in a different calling. She could be a teenager or an elderly widow. The Bible gives us examples of strong women who served as prophets, intercessors, judges, and teachers. "Many women do noble [*chayil*] things," Proverbs 31:29 reminds us. The "many women" in this verse are not mentioned by name, leaving room for us to reflect upon the variety of women of valor throughout the Bible, along with personal examples from our own lives.

It's important to keep in mind that *chayil*, or "valor," is a military term. We can learn many lessons from the battlefield. Marines are instructed that when danger hits, they must run toward, not away from, the danger. And they're told to stick together with their comrades. The Bible reminds us "the wicked flee though no one pursues, but the righteous are as bold as a lion" (Proverbs 28:1). If we want to be women of valor who change our world, we must learn to boldly run toward the hurting and broken of this world—not away from them. But like the Marines, we dare not try this alone.

Word Study

My "valor quest" began with these words: *eshet chayil*. The Hebrew word *eshet* means "woman." The word *chayil* is often translated *valor*. Let's look at the complete definition of *chayil* from the *Hebrew-Greek Key Word Study Bible*: "Might, strength, power, able, valiant, virtuous, army, host, forces, riches, substance, wealth. Primarily signifies military might."[2]

Eshet Chayil

The word *chayil* is used nearly 100 times in the Old Testament. Let's look at the three places the Hebrew term *eshet chayil*, or "woman of valor," is used:

- "Who can find an *eshet chayil* (a woman of valor)?...For her worth is far above rubies" (Proverbs 31:10 OJB).

- "A wife of noble character [*eshet chayil*] is her husband's crown, but a disgraceful wife is like decay in his bones" (Proverbs 12:4).

- "Now my daughter, do not be afraid! Everything you propose, I will do for you, for everyone in town knows that you are a woman of valor" (Ruth 3:11 TLV).

Chayil

Let look at some examples of how *chayil* is used:

- "The angel of the LORD appeared to [Gideon] and said to him, "The LORD is with you, O mighty man of valor" (Judges 6:12 ESV).

- "You armed me with strength [*chayil*] for battle; you humbled my adversaries before me" (Psalm 18:39).

- "They helped David against the band of raiders, for they were all mighty men of valor and were commanders in the army" (1 Chronicles 12:21 ESV).

I hope you are beginning to understand what a powerful term *chayil* is and why it's important that we not lose sight of its full meaning of *eshet chayil* when reading our passage from Proverbs 31.

Prayerful Reading

First, reread the Hebrew version of "A Woman of Valor" poem on pages 33-34 in chapter 1. This is read or sung to Jewish women every Friday night at the Shabbat meal.[3]

Now prayerfully read and reflect on the complete passage below from the Amplified Bible. I have inserted "woman of valor" into verse 10. I found it helped me to read Proverbs 31:10-31 (AMPC) each day during my study. Every time I read the passage, I gained valuable new insights:

> 10 A capable, intelligent, and virtuous woman [woman of valor][4]—who is he who can find her? She is far more precious than jewels and her value is far above rubies or pearls.
>
> 11 The heart of her husband trusts in her confidently and relies on and believes in her securely, so that he has no lack of [honest] gain or need of [dishonest] spoil.
>
> 12 She comforts, encourages, and does him only good as long as there is life within her.
>
> 13 She seeks out wool and flax and works with willing hands [to develop it].
>
> 14 She is like the merchant ships loaded with foodstuffs; she brings her household's food from a far [country].
>
> 15 She rises while it is yet night and gets [spiritual] food for her household and assigns her maids their tasks.
>
> 16 She considers a [new] field before she buys or accepts it [expanding prudently and not courting neglect of her present duties by assuming other duties]; with her savings [of time and strength] she plants fruitful vines in her vineyard.
>
> 17 She girds herself with strength [spiritual, mental, and physical fitness for her God-given task] and makes her arms strong and firm.
>
> 18 She tastes and sees that her gain from work [with and for God] is good; her lamp goes not out, but it burns on continually through the night [of trouble, privation, or sorrow, warning away fear, doubt, and distrust].
>
> 19 She lays her hands to the spindle, and her hands hold the distaff.
>
> 20 She opens her hand to the poor, yes, she reaches out her filled hands to the needy [whether in body, mind, or spirit].

21 She fears not the snow for her family, for all her household are doubly clothed in scarlet.

22 She makes for herself coverlets, cushions, and rugs of tapestry. Her clothing is of linen, pure and fine, and of purple [such as that of which the clothing of the priests and the hallowed cloths of the temple were made].

23 Her husband is known in the [city's] gates, when he sits among the elders of the land.

24 She makes fine linen garments and leads others to buy them; she delivers to the merchants girdles [or sashes that free one up for service].

25 Strength and dignity are her clothing and her position is strong and secure; she rejoices over the future [the latter day or time to come, knowing that she and her family are in readiness for it]!

26 She opens her mouth in skillful and godly Wisdom, and on her tongue is the law of kindness [giving counsel and instruction].

27 She looks well to how things go in her household, and the bread of idleness (gossip, discontent, and self-pity) she will not eat.

28 Her children rise up and call her blessed (happy, fortunate, and to be envied); and her husband boasts of and praises her, [saying],

29 Many daughters have done virtuously, nobly, and well [with the strength of character that is steadfast in goodness], but you excel them all.

30 Charm and grace are deceptive, and beauty is vain [because it is not lasting], but a woman who reverently and worshipfully fears the Lord, she shall be praised!

31 Give her of the fruit of her hands, and let her own works praise her in the gates [of the city]!

Reflection Questions

- Why do you think God chose *eshet chayil* to describe the Proverbs 31 woman?

- What verses from Proverbs 31:10-31 speak to your heart? Write them in your journal.

- As you read this passage, do you see an area where you'd like to grow stronger?

- Why do you think the Bible stresses both the nurturer and warrior roles? Do you see yourself as more of a nurturer or a warrior?

- When you think back to your childhood, does a memory (such as my Baby Kitten, Winchester rifle story) describe you as a young girl?

- What do you think of when you hear the term "holy discontent"?[5]

- Did you observe injustice in an experience in your past? How did it make you feel?

Prayer

I challenge you to pray this dangerous prayer and then watch God begin to work: *"Lord, break my heart for what breaks Yours."*

2

She Makes Herself Strong

God is near to the brokenhearted. He loves us when we're weak. But He delights in making us strong. I'm reminded of a story of when David and his men return from a battle, horrified to find their village burned and their wives and children taken captive. They "wept aloud until they had no strength left to weep" (1 Samuel 30:4). Can you imagine the despair? "But David strengthened himself in the LORD his God" (verse 6 ESV).

After seeking the Lord, David receives this answer: "Pursue, for you shall surely overtake and shall surely rescue" (1 Samuel 30:8 ESV). David and his men defeated their enemies and returned with all their family members safe and sound.

How do you strengthen yourself in the Lord? Being strong is crucial to warfare—especially those battles we should be winning. Battles for our marriages, our children, and our communities.

We've learned that the Proverbs 31 woman of valor is not only courageous; she is also strong. "Strength and honour are her clothing" (Proverbs 31:25 KJV). And "she dresses herself with strength and makes her arms strong" (verse 17 ESV).

But as we learned from Esther, we need to stay dependent on the Lord for our strength. Stay thirsty for Him. Stick together with our community of believers. And stand our ground in the faith.

But some areas of sin and weakness sometimes trip us up and keep us from being strong in our walk with the Lord. The Bible encourages us to be ruthless in getting rid of whatever weighs us down:

Prayerful Reading

- "Let us throw off everything that hinders and the sin that so easily entangles. And let us run with perseverance the

race marked out for us, fixing our eyes on Jesus, the pio-
neer and perfecter of faith" (Hebrews 12:1-2).

- "Rid yourselves of all malice and all deceit, hypocrisy, envy,
  and slander of every kind. Like newborn babies, crave pure
  spiritual milk, so that by it you may grow up in your salvation, now that you have tasted that the Lord is good"
  (1 Peter 2:1-3).

- For additional study, I would encourage you to read the
  short book of Esther this week. Ask the Lord for further
  insights from her example.

Reflection Questions

- Be honest with yourself. What hinders your walk with the
  Lord? Do areas of sin entangle you?

- Do you need to confess any habits that rob your strength?

- How could you become more intentional to "throw off"
  whatever slows you down? Perhaps it would help to have
  an accountability partner or be in a small group.

- Are you bound by anxiety? Remember that the Bible lists
  the "worries of this life" and says "the deceitfulness of
  wealth and the desires for other things come in and choke
  the word, making it unfruitful" (Mark 4:19).

Practice

I encourage you to try a partial or all-day fasting and prayer time.
I've found fasting to be a good way to "stay thirsty" for God and draw
close to Him in prayer. I'm not quite sure why fasting works—I just
know it does. One friend, who calls me her "prayer coach," planned to
try her first full-day fast and asked me for some tips. Here are two tips
that might help you with your fast:

1. **Stay hydrated:** It's my number one secret to effective fasting. I drink a lemon water recipe recommended by a naturopathic doctor: Squeeze the juice of 4-5 lemons into a pitcher of pure water and add 3 tablespoons of pure maple syrup. My doctor friend says this helps regulate blood sugar. Sip on this all day, making sure you get the recommended 8 glasses of water. I have a cup of green tea or two first thing in the morning to avoid getting one of those nasty little caffeine-withdrawal headaches.

2. **Pray when the urge for food hits:** When I feel hunger pangs, that's my alarm bell to pray. I take extra time to read and meditate on the Bible. I rest a little more. Fasting heightens my spiritual sensitivity and seems to propel my prayers in ways I don't understand.

When someone I care about has a pressing problem, it's almost instinctive to fast. I fast when I'm seeking the Lord's guidance. Or when I need for Him to reveal sin in my life. Or sometimes when I just plain feel stuck. Remember, God is pleased when we fast and pray for those who are being oppressed. God says in Isaiah, "This is the kind of fasting I want: Free those who are wrongly imprisoned...Let the oppressed go free, and remove the chains that bind people" (Isaiah 58:6 NLT). Fasting and prayer are one way we can share in the suffering of others, such as persecuted believers around the world.

Prayer

Suffering makes me thirsty for You, Lord, so I turn those worries and burdens into an opportunity to seek You wholeheartedly. Your Word tells me if I draw near to You, then You will draw near to me. Fill me with Your peace and joy. As I humble myself in Your sight, I trust You will lift me up (James 4:8-10).

3

She Laughs at the Future

I do not like heights. Now, I'm fine in an airplane. But if the ground beneath my feet is wobbly (such as the Mile High Swinging Bridge in the mountains of North Carolina), or if there is not a guardrail, I'm a mess. However, I was once towed in a parasail on vacation because I sensed God was urging me on.

In my Bible reading that morning, I had been learning about how we, as believers, are somehow mysteriously seated with Christ in heaven, even while we live on earth: "God raised us up with Christ and seated us with him in the heavenly realms in Christ Jesus" (Ephesians 2:6).

I had been reflecting on how being up that high in the heavenly realm surely affects our view of the earthly realm where we live. I wondered if our problems looked smaller from God's altitude.

Later that same day at the beach, friends invited us go parasailing with them. Yikes! That was high up. But suddenly it hit me. This was my chance to look down on the earth while seated way up high in the heavenlies. Just as I had envisioned in my quiet time that morning. How could I refuse? So I went. And here is what I observed:

To my surprise, it was not scary being gently lifted up to the sky. It helped that I was seated and securely strapped in. I was not literally seated next to Jesus, of course. But David was a good seatmate. As we glided through the air, looking down on the aqua-colored water below, more words from my Bible reading that morning came alive:

> He raised Christ from the dead and seated him at his right hand in the heavenly realms, far above all rule and authority, power and dominion, and every name that is invoked, not only in the present age but also in the one to come. And God placed all things under his feet and appointed

him to be head over everything for the church, which is his body (Ephesians 1:20-23).

Then a curious thing happened. I could see some of the "scary" creatures down below in that water. I saw something that looked like a stingray, and maybe a shark—but they looked very small beneath my feet, which were dangling from the chair. Yes, I was "seated above" the enemies, and they were literally under my feet.

I wondered if that's how we are to look upon the devil and his minions, and the evil of this world. From our position on high, seated with Jesus, we are a glorious spectator to God's work in the world. We don't have to live in continual fear and anxiety!

Perhaps our Proverbs 31 woman, who had such a close relationship with the Lord, had this kind of heavenly perspective. Over the years, she must have learned to look at her life from God's vantage point. Therefore, she could "laugh at the days to come" (Proverbs 31:25).

Connection to Thanksgiving

Being seated in the heavenly places with Jesus is a good reason to give thanks. In chapter 3, we saw the connection between thanksgiving, praise, and joy. When we lift our hearts in praise and thanksgiving, it's as though God then lifts us up to see life (and our problems) from His point of view. That brings joy. Sometimes it's good to be reminded of just how powerful Jesus truly is.

Prayerful Reading

- "Rejoice always, pray without ceasing, give thanks in all circumstances; for this is the will of God in Christ Jesus for you" (1 Thessalonians 5:16-18 esv).

- "Devote yourselves to prayer, being watchful and thankful" (Colossians 4:2).

- "Taking the five loaves and the two fish and looking up
  to heaven, he gave thanks and broke them. Then he gave
  them to the disciples to distribute to the people. They all
  [5000] ate and were satisfied" (Luke 9:16-17).

Reflection Questions

- Why do you think thanksgiving so often seems to precede
  a miracle in the Bible? For example, Jesus thanked God
  before raising Lazarus (John 11:41) and feeding the multi-
  tude (Luke 9:16).

- How does it make you feel when your children are grateful? When they are not?

- How could you be more intentional to show gratitude to
  those closest to you?

Practice

Let's try an experiment in being thankful. For one week, try to
make thankfulness your "go to" response—even in frustrations. I did
this recently when walking through a tough time with a family member.

1. **Giving thanks to God** is a good counterattack. It's easier
   to replace grumbling or complaining with thanksgiving
   than to simply try not to gripe.

2. **Gratitude feeds my faith.** I've learned that thanksgiving
   can stand up under fiery trials. Giving thanks uses less
   energy than praying for a specific end—a good thing when
   you're going through a tough time.

3. **Giving thanks helps** me roll my burdens into God's
   hands, which calms my anxious heart.

4. **Having a thankful heart** makes me more aware of my surroundings and more in touch with God's blessings. I find myself more expectant—watching for Him to show up.

5. **Giving thanks makes me more sensitive** to the needs of others—opening the door to holy conversations—a blessing in themselves.

Final Thoughts on This Chapter

There's daily evidence of God's grace all around us, if only we'll take the time to notice. I had a friend whose teenage daughter did just that. She kept a gratitude journal—her "thank-you book," she called it. At first she could find only a few things each day for which to be thankful. But as she continued to practice thankfulness, her list began to number in the hundreds. I watched her personality blossom and grow until the young lady radiated joy. Maybe you want to keep your own thank-you book or have a section in your journal for a thank-you list. I wonder if you, too, will experience God in a fresh way when you practice gratitude.

Prayer

Lord, I see now that thankfulness and joy are connected. I confess how easily I slip into a habit of complaining. I ask You to help me form a new habit: that of having a thankful heart.

4

She Builds Her House Wisely

The Pew Research Center recently found that "being good parents" and "having a successful marriage" were the millennial generation's top two aspirations.[6] It's good to know family still matters to generation next. In my conversations with women, I'm hearing a recurring theme—their heart's desire to be strong for their families and communities.

As we learned, the Bible words for *house* and *home* are interchangeable with the word for *family*. When a woman builds her home, literally and figuratively, she is building her family. Whether she is married, single, or widowed, a woman has the unique ability to build up those in her community of faith.

The Proverbs 31 woman lived an ordinary life, but with great faithfulness, love, excellence, and kindness. Her life and her works brought the rewards of recognition from her family and community. According to her husband, "Many women have done noble [*chayil*] and valiant things," but this woman's life "surpassed them all' (Proverbs 31:29, paraphrased).

Guard Yourself and Your Families

Today's world is hard on marriage, and the family in particular. The verses below talk about how we can guard our homes and families. But the Bible also encourages us to build strong relationships in the body of Christ and guard them with the same diligence.

Prayerful Reading

- "Encourage one another and build each other up, just as in fact you are doing" (1 Thessalonians 5:11).

- "Do we not all have one Father? Did not one God create us? Why do we profane the covenant of our ancestors by being unfaithful to one another?" (Malachi 2:10).

- "You cover the LORD's altar with tears, with weeping and groaning because he no longer regards the offering or accepts it with favor from your hand. But you say, 'Why does he not?' Because the LORD was witness between you and the wife of your youth, to whom you have been faithless, though she is your companion and your wife by covenant. Did he not make them one, with a portion of the Spirit in their union? And what was the one God seeking? Godly offspring. *So guard yourselves in your spirit*, and let none of you be faithless to the wife of your youth. 'For the man who does not love his wife but divorces her, says the LORD, the God of Israel, covers his garment with violence, says the LORD of hosts. *So guard yourselves in your spirit,* and do not be faithless'" (Malachi 2:13-16 ESV, emphasis mine).

- "Likewise, teach the older women to be reverent in the way they live, not to be slanderers or addicted to much wine, but to teach what is good. Then they can urge the younger women to love their husbands and children, to be self-controlled and pure, to be busy at home, to be kind, and to be subject to their husbands, so that no one will malign the word of God" (Titus 2:3-5).

Malachi 2:13-16 is addressed to husbands. But with 70 percent of divorces now initiated by women, it makes sense for women to be especially mindful to heed these verses.

Reflection Questions

- Based on what we have been learning, what are some ways to "guard [yourself] in your spirit" in your marriage?

- Malachi 2:10 talks about being "unfaithful" to our brothers and sisters in the faith. How might you "guard [yourself] in your spirit" in those relationships too?

- What are some ways to "build each other up?" Look at the MOUNCE version of 1 Thessalonians 5:11 for additional study (on BibleGateway.com).[7]

- Titus 2 tells us the Word of God can be maligned when families fail. In a positive way, how could a strong family honor God's reputation among unbelievers?

Practice

We talked about "temple upkeep" in chapter 4. Taking care of our physical bodies affects our minds and emotions, and especially our relationships. Even our spiritual lives suffer when our bodies are a wreck. Healthy food, rest, water, recreation. Remember, you're training yourself to sustain yourself. Here are some tips to help you care for that temple:

- Use this easy method for getting enough pure water: Take a 16-ounce cup—the sports game cups work. Drink a full 16 ounces of pure water upon rising each morning. Then another around mid-morning, another around mid-afternoon, and one more before bedtime. Voila. Your 64 ounces per day. If you don't follow this hydrating plan, you'll only sip your beverage at meals. But too much water at mealtime dilutes digestive juices and impairs digestion.

- Find one of the countless plans for eating healthy. Lower your carbs. Cut out most sugar. Eat lots of fresh fruits, veggies, and lean meat. Just do it.

- I mentioned a half-hour fast walk or jog outdoors five times a week. This helps depression and anxiety, because over time it raises your serotonin levels. You'll get your vitamin D. Take your Chubby Book for prayer and reflection on your walk. It's kind of a spiritual follow-up to your morning quiet time. Or maybe you just want to unwind while you walk.

- Get away for little overnighters with your husband, or take mini-vacations with friends.

- Start a vacation line item in your budget and put money aside every month. Then *take* your vacations.

- My favorite way to unwind at the end of the day with my hubby is doing this: Prepare organic popcorn in a hot-air popper (Presto has them for under twenty dollars). Melt 2 tablespoons coconut oil and a teensy bit of organic butter. Drizzle warmed oil over freshly popped corn. Top with sea salt. We like to split a bar of dark chocolate too. Yummy and pretty healthy!

- Don't forget my friend Beth's 100-push-ups-a-day plan!

- Remember the Sabbath! The Jewish people sometimes refer to this as a little bit of heaven on earth.

- Watch what you put in your mind. God put Philippians 4:8 in the Bible for a good reason.

Prayer

Lord, You created me to require rest each day. You even ordained a special Sabbath for me to enjoy my relationships with You and those I love. My faith flourishes when I enter into Your rest. Remind me to celebrate Your precious gift of rest (Hebrews 4:1-11).

5

She Prays Hard

I seem to talk a lot about waiting since waiting was such a part of my life when we were walking through infertility. But waiting is a normal part of anyone's life. Are you waiting for something? Maybe it's the fulfillment of a dream or the resolution of a long-standing problem. You're waiting for a spouse, or a baby, or a wayward child to come home. Or you're anxiously awaiting a medical diagnosis, waiting for healing, waiting for hope. Whatever you're waiting for, I'm sure you agree that waiting is hard work. The Bible encourages us to wait for hope with endurance. What does it mean to wait with endurance?

We've emphasized the importance of training our hearts to hear God's voice and learning to abide in Christ daily. It turns out there is a strong connection between abiding and waiting with endurance.

Prayerful Reading

- "If we hope for what we do not see, we eagerly wait for it with endurance" (Romans 8:25 NET).

- "If you abide in me, and my words abide in you, ask whatever you wish, and it will be done for you" (John 15:7 ESV).

Word Study

hypomeno

We discover an interesting secret by looking at the Greek word *hypomeno*, translated *endure*. It comes from two words: *hypo* or "under" and *meno* or "abide". *Meno* is the same word Jesus uses when He encourages us to *abide* in Him.

So *hypomeno*, or *endure*, is to "abide under" a time of trial as we wait for hope. This kind of endurance is a quality of mind that enables us to "suffer with a tranquil mind."[8] Bottom line? We learn to endure as we "abide under" our circumstances and "abide in" Christ during our times of waiting. Abiding helps us hold on to hope. It helps us wait with endurance.

Reflection Questions

- Will you be able to stand your ground during times of trouble? If we're faithful to abide in Christ daily when life is going well, then we'll be more likely to endure when those inevitable storms of life hit.

- What does abiding look like for you? Ponder this thought: Abiding in Jesus helps you endure as you wait for hope.

Practice

I've stressed the importance of developing a pattern for prayer and reading God's Word. I'm always on the lookout to find practical ways to abide in Christ. When I was a new believer, I came across a format that challenged me to set aside 21 days to read the Gospel of John. John has 21 chapters, so it works well to read a chapter a day. Many people have even come to faith simply by reading John's Gospel.

I periodically use this simple spiritual exercise to revive my own faith. You can even use this experiment to jump-start your process of keeping a list in your Chubby Book. Each time I perform my own 21-Day Experiment,[9] God speaks to me in a tangible way. I like to use this simple format every day no matter which book of the Bible I happen to be reading.

The 21-Day Experiment
Ground Rules:

- Make a decision to stick with this 21-Day Experiment. Don't evaluate whether any changes occur until the end of the 21 days. You can even say to yourself, *Well, nothing seems to be happening today, but I will postpone judging its impact until after 21 days.*

- Remember that the main purpose of the experiment is for Jesus to become more real to you and for God's Word to come alive. Answered prayer is a by-product.

The Daily Format:

1. Set aside 15 minutes each day to prayerfully read one chapter of John's Gospel.

2. Pray for God to impress a verse or two upon your mind for that day. Write that "watchword" on your 3 x 5-inch card in your Chubby Book.

3. On the adjacent card, write that day's needs from your prayer list.

4. Inspired by what you read from John, pray for your prayer list. Sometimes I will pray the verse from John as a promise for that person.

5. Pray over this list again as you go for a walk, do dishes, or drive in your car. Sometimes I meditate on or memorize the verse from that day's reading.

6. Pray for God to help you notice subtle answers throughout the day. Psalm 5:3 says, "Morning by morning I lay my requests before You, Lord, and eagerly watch for the answers" (paraphrased).

A Final Thought on This Chapter

At the end of your 21-Day Experiment, spend some time reflecting on what you've observed. Have you noticed God at work in your life? Are you more in tune with His voice? Sometimes it helps to have a friend do this experiment with you. The accountability is good. You may discover, like I did, that having a prayer partner to "agree" with you in prayer is powerful.

Prayer

> *Lord, Your Word is powerful. It fills me with love, courage, strength, faith, joy—whatever I need at the moment. Draw me to Your Word. Let Your Word become my rock-solid foundation.*

6

She Dares to Dream Big

Our God-given dreams can affect the entire direction of our lives. My young friend Dominique was just ten when some gang members befriended him. "I was kind of a mascot," he says. But gang mascots eventually become gang members, and he was headed for trouble. One day Dominique discovered an online chess game. He got the hang of it and became good—really good. Before too long, he was "busy" when gang members called. Dominique was way too busy finding his purpose to run with gangs.

By the time he was in high school, Dominique had become the top scholastic chess player in the state of North Carolina. In his college application, Dominique wrote, "By getting closer to the One who allowed me this chance, and continuing with the plan that we dreamed up together when I was a young child, I feel that I will be able to help someone else and make a lasting impact."

Dominique didn't attend church growing up. But as a small child he had a sense of God's destiny and a mysterious awareness of His calling through his childhood dreams of playing chess. And when he heard a clear presentation of the gospel his first semester in college, the vibrant young man accepted Jesus Christ as Lord and Savior. Dominique graduated from college—the first in his family. He continues to play chess and has made his way into the realm of international competition.

One thing is clear: Dominique's earthly dreams had eternal implications that went far beyond the mastery of chess. This is a good reminder to take seriously the hopes and dreams of the children entrusted to our care. Mother Teresa put it this way: "Tread gently around the dreams of a child. You might be treading on the dreams of God."

Prayerful Reading

- "Now to him who is able to do immeasurably more than all we ask or imagine, according to his power that is at work within us, to him be glory in the church and in Christ Jesus throughout all generations" (Ephesians 3:20-21).

- "We know that in all things God works for the good of those who love him, who have been called according to his purpose. For those God foreknew he also predestined to be conformed to the image of his Son...And those he predestined, he also called; those he called, he also justified; those he justified, he also glorified...If God is for us, who can be against us?" (Romans 8:28-31).

- "I am sure of this, that he who began a good work in you will bring it to completion at the day of Jesus Christ" (Philippians 1:6 ESV).

Reflection Questions

- If you have children, do you see signs of their dreams beginning to take shape?

- Did an activity as a child make you think, *I was meant to do this*?

- Are you using that gift or talent in your adult life? Can you incorporate that into a hobby or even volunteer work?

- What obstacles may be keeping your child from reaching his or her dream? Does he or she need assistance, extra training, a supportive team?

- Is anything getting in the way of your own dream?

Practice

We discovered that watching good movies together was a fun way to fuel the fires of our children's dreams (as well as our own). Over the years, I've enjoyed seeing dreams emerge in each of our children's lives. Yes, we have to do the work of developing the skills and talent, getting the right education, and persisting until the necessary doors open. But God has given us such vivid imaginations to help propel us toward our dreams. Good movies can inspire us to ask the question, "What if? What if I followed the example of someone who reached their dream? If they endured all the obstacles, then maybe I could too."

Plus, many movies also deal with themes like endurance, kindness, racial reconciliation, or overcoming tragedy and hardship. We had our list, and now our daughter is adding her list of favorites for her family. Begin to look for inspiring movies—and don't forget the classics. Filmmakers have learned this secret: Dreaming big never goes out of style. Here are a few (not in any particular order) from our family's list of favorites. Check online reviews for themes and suitability for your children's ages and stages.

- *October Sky*
- *Seabiscuit*
- *Rudy*
- *The Pursuit of Happyness*
- *Field of Dreams*
- *Rocky*
- *Soul Surfer*
- *McFarland, USA*

- *Million Dollar Arm*
- *Freedom Writers*
- *Remember the Titans*
- *The Blind Side*
- *The Sound of Music*
- *Mary Poppins*
- *Chariots of Fire*
- *Akeelah and the Bee*
- *The Queen of Katwe*

Prayer

Lord, it's wonderful that You have given us the ability to dream big, and the imaginations to fuel those dreams. Help us to ask, "What if?" and to truly believe that all things are possible with You (Mark 9:23).

7

She Leads with Kindness

Back in high school, I had a secret litmus test to decide if I liked my date. He, of course, never suspected, but I would observe how he treated our waiter or waitress. If he didn't take the time to be kind, the guy was off my list. What's more, I took note how he treated his mother.

Sadly, our culture has become more and more self-centered. Kindness seems to be a lost art. Some believe kindness is too soft for today's dog-eat-dog world. Too tame for our ambitions. Many would tell you kindness is not the pathway to success. Besides, most of us are moving too fast to take the time to be kind to those we encounter every day.

The Bible presents us with a different picture. "A kindhearted woman gains honor, but ruthless men gain only wealth. Those who are kind benefit themselves, but the cruel bring ruin on themselves" (Proverbs 11:16-17).

We've observed that kindness characterized the leadership of Deborah, the Proverbs 31 woman, and others. Kindness carried its own rewards, sometimes opening the door to dreams. Ruth's kindness and devotion to her widowed mother-in-law brought about a destiny that put her squarely in the lineage of Jesus Christ—one of only four women mentioned by name in the genealogy of Jesus, listed in Matthew 1:2-16.

From God's perspective, kindness can have world-changing implications. We've learned that the Hebrew word for "kindness," *chesed*, is considered one of the most important attributes of God. The New Testament also paints a clear picture of the loving-kindness of our heavenly Father.

Prayerful Reading

- "Do you have no regard for the wealth of His kindness and tolerance and patience [in withholding His wrath]? Are you [actually] unaware or ignorant [of the fact] that God's kindness leads you to repentance [that is, to change your inner self, your old way of thinking—seek His purpose for your life]?" (Romans 2:4 AMP).

- "Every good and perfect gift is from above, coming down from the Father of the heavenly lights, who does not change like shifting shadows. He chose to give us birth through the word of truth, that we might be a kind of first-fruits of all he created" (James 1:17-18).

Reflection Questions

- What if God is kind but not powerful?
- What if He is powerful but not loving?
- How do we rest in the knowledge that He is both?
- How does this passage enliven your understanding of God's kindness?

   Because of his great love for us, God, who is rich in mercy, made us alive with Christ even when we were dead in transgressions—it is by grace you have been saved. And God raised us up with Christ and seated us with him in the heavenly realms in Christ Jesus, in order that in the coming ages he might show the incomparable riches of his grace, expressed in his kindness to us in Christ Jesus. For it is by grace you have been saved, through faith—and this is not from yourselves, it is the gift of God (Ephesians 2:4-8).

- Do you think our culture emphasizes kindness too much

or too little? Is kindness without truth beneficial? Why or why not?

- How might kindness open the door to conversations or friendships with those with whom we disagree? A rabbi friend of mine once confided that sometimes Christians lack "non-hostile" ways to express our strong beliefs. I took the words to heart and have tried to be kind and yet speak truth.

- How could you find non-hostile and even kind ways to express your beliefs?

- Does our kindness guarantee that unbelievers will always be receptive to the gospel? Why or why not?

Practice

We learned from our reading in chapter 7 that kindness actually makes people happier. Those who performed acts of kindness, especially to family members, scored the highest.

- Plan five acts of kindness this week for people in your family, starting with your husband if you're married. Or perhaps five random acts for people you don't know.

- If you are going through this study with a prayer partner or group, compare notes about your acts of kindness for the week.

Prayer

Lord, please prompt us how and when to show kindness to others this week, beginning with those closest to us. And give us Your heart for the lost. May our kindness open the door to conversations that may have an eternal impact.

8

She Gives Her Life Away

I was part of a team-building exercise recently at one of those "escape route" venues that have sprung up across the country. The format is pretty much the same in all of them. You and a team of your friends, family, or coworkers choose to be locked together in a "mystery room." Your team has exactly one adrenaline-packed hour to find your way out.

The theme might be a murder mystery, a bank heist, or a space adventure. You have to work hard, work smart, and work together to unravel the clues. You search furiously for a number of hidden keys to locked doors that lead to yet more keys and more clues and more locked doors...and all while the clock is ticking.

Believe me—speaking as one whose team did not make it out in time—the test is daunting. But it's also exhilarating. I can't wait to try it again. I'm pretty sure these places would not be so wildly popular if the challenges were simple and the mysteries easily solved. Part of the thrill is the difficulty of the quest.

A quest can be defined as a long or arduous search for something. Webster adds a colorful flair, defining *quest* as "a chivalrous enterprise in medieval romance usually involving an adventurous journey."[10]

Together, we've been on a quest to explore what the Bible has to say about the woman of valor. We've seen the stories of ordinary women like ourselves. I trust we have taken the time to examine our own lives in the process.

I have encouraged you to ask the Lord to speak to your heart and to help you discover His purpose for your life. As with any adventure, there is always the unexpected. Perhaps the Lord will bring healing of relationships or the restoration of something you have lost while you're on the quest to become a woman of valor.

I remind you that when we find balance in our roles as nurturer and warrior, those around us will best flourish.

Prayerful Reading

- "Just as each of us has one body with many members, and these members do not all have the same function, so in Christ we, though many, form one body, and each member belongs to all the others. We have different gifts, according to the grace given to each of us. If your gift is prophesying, then prophesy in accordance with your faith; if it is serving, then serve; if it is teaching, then teach; if it is to encourage, then give encouragement; if it is giving, then give generously; if it is to lead, do it diligently; if it is to show mercy, do it cheerfully" (Romans 12:4-8).

- "God is able to bless you abundantly, so that in all things at all times, having all that you need, you will abound in every good work" (2 Corinthians 9:8).

Reflection Questions

- What is your holy discontent?
- How did God answer this prayer: "Break my heart for what breaks Yours"?
- How might you take a small step today?
- Keep asking: How should I pray? What can I give? Where should I go?
- Reflect on the ways your life experiences, even your trials, have prepared you to respond to God's call.

Practice

- Consider whether training or an area of study would help you grow in your gifts.

- Explore ways to partner with a local church or others in your community who are serving in a way that inspires you.

- Take one of the many online spiritual gifts tests to help you unlock your gifts.

- Just go!

Prayer

Dear friend, my prayer is that you're beginning to discover that you are a woman of valor. God has given you the strength and courage you need for His calling. My guess is your life experiences have already prepared you well. Don't be afraid of your broken places, for that's where God sometimes shines brightest. And may you find the true fulfillment that comes as you pour your life out for others.

9

She Is Destined to Reign

Now that you've completed the book, I encourage you to spend some time alone with the Lord. Maybe even a half-day retreat to reflect on what you've learned. I've given you a lot to think about. Now it's time to make it personal. God has provided the strength and courage you need to step out in faith as a woman of valor.

My prayer is that you're beginning to see yourself as God sees you. Yes, He created you to be a woman of valor. What's more, when you accept Jesus, you are destined to reign with Him. That means you are part nurturer, part warrior, and part *royalty*.

The Bible tells us that we are mysteriously grafted into Christ's position of power and authority. We are a royal priesthood!

What an amazing thought. God has created us with the gifts, ability, power, and royal position to reign with Christ. Both in this life, and throughout eternity!

The word *reign* comes from a Latin word that means king, or kingdom. A dictionary search of the word *reign* yields a variety of definitions:

- To hold royal office as a king or queen
- To exercise authority
- To predominate, to prevail
- To rule or govern
- To have widespread influence

Just think. As believers, and as women of valor, God has called us to exercise His authority. To prevail over evil. To rule and govern. To have widespread influence.

Let's see what the Bible says about our destiny:

Prayerful Reading

We are destined to reign in this life:

- For if, while we were God's enemies, we were reconciled to him through the death of his Son, how much more, having been reconciled, shall we be saved through his life!... For if, by the trespass of the one man, death **reigned** through that one man, how much more will those who receive God's abundant provision of grace and of the gift of righteousness **reign in life** through the one man, Jesus Christ! (Romans 5:10,17).

We are to reign over sin, not let it reign over us:

- Therefore do not let sin **reign** in your mortal body so that you obey its evil desires. Do not offer any part of yourself to sin as an instrument of wickedness, but rather offer yourselves to God as those who have been brought from death to life; and offer every part of yourself to him as an instrument of righteousness. For sin shall no longer be your master, because you are not under the law, but under grace (Romans 6:12-14).

We are destined to reign in eternity:

- The throne of God and of the Lamb will be in the city, and his servants will serve him. They will see his face, and his name will be on their foreheads. There will be no more night. They will not need the light of a lamp or the light of the sun, for the Lord God will give them light. And they will **reign** for ever and ever (Revelation 22:3-5).

Reflection Questions

- God's Word says you are not only a woman of valor, but also a woman of royalty. How does this impact your view of yourself?

- Is there an area of sin or weakness you would like to "reign over" in your life? Fear, addiction, idolatry, jealousy, a critical or judgmental spirit, worry?

- What lessons did you learn from Esther and others about how to defeat evil and stand up to the enemy?

- How does your understanding of Christ's authority working through you impact your view of spiritual warfare? Of prayer?

A Final Thought

- We've emphasized the importance of learning to abide in Christ. The Bible teaches us that even our ability to reign is connected to abiding : "If we endure, we will also **reign** with him" (2 Timothy 2:12). The word translated "endure" is *hyponeno,* or "to abide under." (We studied the connection between *abiding* and *enduring* in chapter 5).

- Do you see how abiding in Christ is a thread running through this entire book? The woman of valor—the one destined to reign—is the woman who fears the Lord, who makes Him her refuge, her ruler, her Savior, her friend, her home.

- Our gifts, our talents, our good works, even our royalty, all flow out of our relationship with Jesus. What's more, when we live as women of valor, walking in royalty, we are actually preparing for our eternity. I guess you could say we are "training for reigning."

Prayer

Lord, give me courage to step out in faith as a woman of valor. Teach me that as I abide, I will reign with You. Thank You for the awesome privilege of starting the work I will do for all eternity! Help me not to tarry…but to take a small step to begin today! I believe You are calling me for such a time as this.

Notes

What Is a Woman of Valor?

1. My husband, David, and I have recently written companion books where we explore ways this lost art of honor can be reclaimed in our marriages, our families, and our culture. See Marilynn Chadwick, *Eight Great Ways to Honor Your Husband* (Eugene, OR: Harvest House, 2016) and David Chadwick, *Eight Great Ways to Honor Your Wife* (Eugene, OR: Harvest House, 2016).

Chapter 1: She Is a Fierce Fighter

1. JPS; The Bible text designated "JPS Old Testament (1917)" is from the Jewish Publication Society's English translation of the Hebrew Old Testament published in 1917.

2. Marilynn Chadwick, *Eight Great Ways to Honor Your Husband* (Eugene, OR: Harvest House, 2016). David Chadwick, *Eight Great Ways to Honor Your Wife* (Eugene, OR: Harvest House, 2016).

3. Spiros Zodhiates, ed., *Hebrew-Greek Key Word Study Bible*, NIV (Chattanooga, TN: AMG Publishers, 1996), 1515.

4. Genesis 3:14-15 (NIV): "So the Lord God said to the serpent, 'Because you have done this…I will put enmity between you and the woman, and between your offspring and hers; he will crush your head, and you will strike his heel.'"

5. The poem as translated from Hebrew, adapted from Proverbs 31:10-31; http://www.aish.com/sh/ht/fn/48966686.html

Chapter 2: She Makes Herself Strong

1. https://godswordtowomen.org/virtuous.htm

2. http://www.merriam-webster.com/dictionary/virtue, The Merriam-Webster Online Dictionary is based on the print version of *Merriam-Webster's Collegiate® Dictionary, Eleventh Edition.*

3. http://www.etymonline.com/index.php?allowed_in_frame=0&search=virtue

4. https://www.biblegateway.com/quicksearch/?search=virtue&version=WYC&searchtype=all

5. You can read more about my journey in prayer: Marilynn Chadwick, *Sometimes He Whispers, Sometimes He Roars: Learning to Hear the Voice of God* (New York: Howard Books, 2012).

6. *Isolation sickness*: https://socialwellness.wordpress.com/why-social-isolation-makes-us-sick—a-theory/

Chapter 3: She Laughs at the Future

1. Spiros Zodhiates, ed., *Hebrew-Greek Key Word Study Bible*, NIV (Chattanooga, TN: AMG Publishers, 1996), 2016.

2. Brené Brown at TEDxHouston; https://www.youtube.com/watch?v=X4Qm9cGRub0

3. Marilynn Chadwick, *Sometimes He Whispers, Sometimes He Roars: Learning to Hear the Voice of God* (New York; Howard Books, 2012).

4. Charles H. Spurgeon, *The Power of Prayer in a Believer's Life*, complied and edited by Robert Hall (Lynn, WA: Emerald Books, 1993), 168.

5. https://www.youtube.com/watch?v=UuuZMg6NVeA

6. *The United Methodist Hymnal,* Number 110; Text: *Martin Luther,* Trans. by Frederick H. Hedge; Music: Martin Luther Harmony from The New Hymnal for American Youth.

7. Mike Mason, *Champagne for the Soul* (Colorado Springs: Waterbrook Press, 2003), 44-45.

Chapter 4: She Builds Her House Wisely

1. http://liveactionnews.org/olympics-star-kerri-walsh-jennings-born-babies-play-volleyball/

2. http://alpine.usskiteam.com/news/vonn-releases-strong-new-beautiful

3. Judges 5:7; Judges 4:5.

4. http://forward.com/sisterhood/209716/a-woman-of-valor-who-will-find-check-her-hair/

5. http://www.heritage.org/research/reports/2012/09/marriage-americas-greatest-weapon-against -child-poverty

6. Calculated from data in U.S. Bureau of the Census, American Community Survey, 2007–2009, http://factfinder2.census.gov/faces/tableservices/jsf/pages/productview .xhtml?pid=ACS_09_3YR_S1702&prodType=table

7. Robert Rector and Kirk A. Johnson, Ph.D., "The Effects of Marriage and Maternal Education in Reducing Child Poverty," Heritage Foundation, *Center for Data Analysis Report* No. 02-05, August 2, 2002.

8. https://www.billmounce.com/greek-dictionary/oikodomeo

9. http://www.merriam-webster.com/dictionary/nurture

10. I discuss honor and respect in greater depth in *Eight Great Ways to Honor Your Husband* (Eugene, OR: Harvest House, 2016).

11. James Dobson, *Hide or Seek* (Old Tappan, NJ: Fleming H. Revell, 1974).

12. Mission of Hope, Haiti: Housing Projects: http://www.mohhaiti.org

13. http://www.huffingtonpost.com/eve-blossom/haiti-human-trafficking-o_b_436412.html

Chapter 5: She Prays Hard

1. ALARM was founded by Dr. Celestin Musekura, survivor of the Rwandan genocide. Learn more about ALARM at: http://www.alarm-inc.org

2. David Chadwick, *It's How You Play the Game* (Eugene, OR, Harvest House, 2015).

3. https://billmounce.com/greek-dictionary/meno

4. Marilynn Chadwick, *Sometimes He Whispers, Sometimes He Roars: Learning to Hear the Voice of God* (New York: Howard Books, 2012).

5. https://billmounce.com/greek-dictionary/logos

Chapter 6: She Dares to Dream Big

1. http://biblehub.com/hebrew/6965.htm

2. Spiros Zodhiates, ed., *Hebrew-Greek Key Word Study Bible,* NIV (Chattanooga, TN: AMG Publishers, 1996), 1595.

Chapter 7: She Leads with Kindness

1. Spiros Zodhiates, ed., *Hebrew-Greek Key Word Study Bible,* NIV (Chattanooga, TN: AMG Publishers, 1996), 1687.

2. Amanda Foreman, "Why Footbinding Persisted in China for a Millennium." *The Smithsonian Magazine,* February, 2015, Smithsonian.com. http://www.smithsonianmag.com/history/why-footbinding-persisted-china-millennium-180953971/?no-ist

3. http://www.todayifoundout.com/index.php/2015/05/women-fainted-much-19th-century/

4. http://abcnews.go.com/blogs/health/2013/03/25/thigh-gap-new-teen-body-obsession/

5. https://www.eatingdisorderhope.com/information/statistics-studies

6. Cindi May, "The Problem with Female Superheroes," *Scientific American,* June 2015, http://www.scientificamerican.com/article/the-problem-with-female-superheroes

7. May, Ibid.

8. http://www.dailymail.co.uk/news/article-2165347/Why-ARE-mothers-addicted-ADHD-drug-Adderall-Women-reveal-ve-stolen-drugs-children-pressure-perfect.html

9. http://www.shape.com/lifestyle/mind-and-body/adhd-or-overachiever-women-and-epidemic-adderall-abuse

10. Spiros Zodhiates, ed., *Hebrew-Greek Key Word Study Bible,* NIV (Chattanooga, TN: AMG Publishers, 1996), 1516.

11. *St. Augustine's Confessions,* https://www.crossroadsinitiative.com/media/articles/ourheartisrestlessuntilitrestsinyou/

12. Learn more about Mission India: https://missionindia.org

13. http://www.aish.com/f/mom/48910797.html

Chapter 8: She Gives Her Life Away

1. https://nces.ed.gov/fastfacts/display.asp?id=72

2. Marcus Buckingham, *Find Your Strongest Life* (Nashville: Thomas Nelson, 2009), 16-25.

3. Buckingham, *Find Your Strongest Life,* 26.

4. Go to http://www.fashionandcompassion.com for more information about their mission or to order from their exquisite jewelry and accessories collection.

5. https://www.lynnehybels.com/what-are-we-called-to-die-to/

6. Don and Barb Linsz, *Miracle Beans and the Golden Book* (Charlotte; Mandate Publishing, 2012). The story of their adventures when they left the comforts of home in Ohio and packed up their children to take the gospel into remote areas in Ethiopia.

7. Kerry Walters, "Mother Teresa: "A Saint who Conquered Darkness"; *American Catholic Blog*: July 15, 2016, http://blog.franciscanmedia.org/mother-teresa-a-saint-who-conquered-darkness. This post is an excerpt of Walters' recent book: *St. Teresa of Calcutta: Missionary, Mother, Mystic* (Cincinnati: Franciscan Media, 2016).

8. WBT Radio 1110AM; *The David Chadwick Show*: "Interview with Bishop William Curlin on Canonization Day of Mother Teresa; September 4, 2016, http://wbt.com/episodes/canonization-mother-teresa/ Bishop William Curlin led the Catholic Diocese of Charlotte

from 1994 until his retirement in 2002. He was very close to Mother Teresa for more than 20 years, serving as spiritual advisor to her and the Missionaries of Charity sisters.

9. Gretchen Filz, "Meet the Bishop Mother Teresa Called Her Spiritual Father and Spiritual Son," *Get Fed,* August 24, 2016, https://www.catholiccompany.com/getfed/mother-teresa-spiritual -father/

Chapter 9: She Is Destined to Reign

1. Naomi Wolfe, *The New York Times,* opinion 2012: reprinted from *International Herald Tribune,* December 2011. See http://www.nytimes.com/2011/12/02/opinion/magazine-global-agenda- mommy-i-want-to-be-a-princess.html?pagewanted=all&_r=0

2. Wolfe, *The New York Times.*

3. http://www.rootsweb.ancestry.com/~nwa/margaret.html

4. http://www.catholic.org/saints/saint.php?saint_id=304

5. Spiros Zodhiates, ed., *Hebrew-Greek Key Word Study Bible,* NIV (Chattanooga, TN: AMG Publishers, 1996), 1520.

Valor Quest: Woman of Valor Study Guide

1. As mentioned, this is author and Bible teacher Beth Moore's favorite version. To order, see https://www.amazon.com/Hebrew-Greek-Study-Bible

2. Spiros Zodhiates, ed., *Hebrew-Greek Key Word Study Bible*, NIV (Chattanooga, TN: AMG Publishers, 1996), 1515.

3. http://www.hebrew4christians.com/Blessings/Shabbat_Blessings/Eshet_Chayil/eshet_chayil. html

4. The Hebrew words here are *eshet chayil* so I have bracketed "woman of valor" into this text.

5. Bill Hybels is known for this term, and has even written a book by that title.

6. Pew Research Center, *Confident. Connected. Open to Change*; February 2010, http://www .pewsocialtrends.org/files/2010/10/millennials-confident-connected-open-to-change.pdf

7. https://www.biblegateway.com/passage/?search=1+thess+5%3A11&version=MOUNCE

8. Spiros Zodhiates, ed., *Hebrew-Greek Key Word Study Bible*, NIV (Chattanooga, TN: AMG Publishers, 1996), 1683.

9. Adapted from Marilynn Chadwick, *Sometimes He Whispers, Sometimes He Roars: Learning to Hear the Voice of God* (New York: Howard Books, 2012), 73-82.

10. https://www.merriam-webster.com/dictionary/quest

Bibles Referenced

More from
Marilynn Chadwick

As a wife, you are uniquely able to honor your husband in ways no one else can. Tragically, in today's culture, the idea of honor in the marriage relationship has been lost. It's a key reason so many marriages aren't what they could be. *In Eight Great Ways to Honor Your Husband,* author Marilynn Chadwick shares how you can show this special kind of love:

- become strong
- guard your home
- believe the best
- lighten his load

- build him up
- dream big together
- create a culture of honor

As you honor your husband, you and he will both experience new heights of fulfillment and intimacy—and you'll show others how beautiful the husband-wife union can be when it follows God's design.